Case Studies in Mergers & Acquisitions

by

John D. Sullivan, Ph.D.

authorHOUSE

1663 LIBERTY DRIVE, SUITE 200
BLOOMINGTON, INDIANA 47403
(800) 839-8640
www.authorhouse.com

© 2004 John D. Sullivan, Ph.D.
All Rights Reserved.

No part of this book may be reproduced, stored in a retrieval system, or transmitted by any means without the written permission of the author.

First published by AuthorHouse 07/09/04

ISBN: 1-4184-3844-8 (sc)

Printed in the United States of America
Bloomington, Indiana

This book is printed on acid-free paper.

For John, & Kiersten

Table of Contents

A Note on Case Study 1

Global Investor Publishing 3

Aetna 2000 15

National Medical Care 35

Teradyne 81

Trans World Airlines 107

The Proposed Merger of Hewlett Packard and Compaq Computer 127

MedImmune 151

Willamette 173

Everest Healthcare Services Corporation 187

Laidlaw, Inc. 209

About the Author 237

A Note on Case Study

These cases have been written to provide graduate students with different sets of problems and issues encountered with mergers and acquisitions. Case studies enable students to step into corporate problems and find solutions based on a set series of data.

To successfully find a solution and make a solid recommendation, each case must be read a multiple of times. Be careful not to mix symptoms with real issues. Without identifying the correct issues, any recommendation made will be off the mark. All the information needed to conclude the case is found within the case. It is irrelevant what actually happened. One of the goals of case study is to teach students to use a "business" paradigm when approaching problems.

Global Investor Publishing

In 1998, from their offices in Alexandria, Virginia and Cambridge, Massachusetts, Brad Durham and Dwight Ingalsbe, co-founders and Managing Directors of Global Investor Publishing, watched a series of economic meltdowns that started in Asia and ran rapidly West through Russia. The results in the international economic community were devastating.

With the collapse of the Russian economy, Durham and Ingalsbe feared that their most profitable and lead product, the financial newsletter *Russia Portfolio*, would experience a significant reduction in circulation and possibly bring an end to the five-year-old company.

Within months, large Russian financial institutions either dropped their expensive subscriptions or simply didn't renew because they were ultimately liquidated and ceased to exist. Outside of Russia, subscription renewals, while less dramatic, were also on the decline. The Russian stock market, once the gem of the new capitalist frontier, was in ruin and portfolio managers were pulling out assets and no longer required the sector specific expertise of Global Investor Publishing. The decline in revenue resulted in a net loss of $40,000 for the 4th quarter.

One potential bright spot on the horizon was the launch of the company's new financial newsletter, *Central Europe Portfolio* in 1997 concentrating on the securities markets in the Czech Republic, Hungary, Poland, Romania, and Slovakia and generating approximately $100,000 in revenue. But with the decline of the Russian markets, these economies also faltered dampening sales of the new financial product.

To pull the company back on track Ingalsbe and Durham shifted gears and refocused their attention on a new prospect. While international portfolio managers might not be as interested in Russia specific information, they might be interested in how assets moved in and out of emerging countries and regions. Both had used the data supplied by Ian Wilson, an entrepreneur that had the ability to take large amounts of information and carve it into a usable medium. Maybe this was the time to entertain the possibility of an acquisition of Ian's company, Emerging Market Funds Research, Inc.? The real risk of course was that

John D. Sullivan, Ph.D.

Emerging Market Funds Research or EMFR, was a data company and Durham and Ingalsbe's experience was in publishing. *a vertical merger*

Company Background

In 1995, with a small investment of their own money and an idea to capitalize on the new economy of the former Soviet Union, Brad Durham and Dwight Ingalsbe launched Russia Portfolio, an objective newsletter geared towards financial institutions and fund managers to assist them in decision making about the Russian securities markets. So valued was this information that in a 1997 interview with the Boston Business Journal, Michael Claudon, professor of economics at Middlebury College said, "Russia Portfolio's analysis of the securities market is almost without equal."[1]

With the change from communism to capitalism, money rushed into the Russian stock market providing triple digit returns and creating more and more investment opportunities as financial institutions created hedge funds and mutual funds with the entire focus and objective tied to the Russian economy.

timing

Riding the wave through 1997, Global Investor Publishing saw its revenue climb to $440,000 providing income of $147,000 before the global economic bubble burst.

Not quite feeling the financial effects of the global economic meltdown, Durham closed the Virginia office and moved to Boston, consolidating the corporate offices. But in that that same year, while the financial performance started out well, by the 4th quarter it had deteriorated considerably leaving revenue slightly below the previous year at $380,000 and a net loss of $40,000 in the last quarter. Several institutional clients either couldn't afford the $1,075 subscription or didn't financially survive the region's economic correction.

With the Russian situation continuing to rapidly deteriorate, the International Monetary Fund stepped in with a series of loans to help ease the sliding ruble. Most of the loans were initially used to

---

[1] Marsha Zabarsky. "The Last Great Play." <u>Boston Business Journal.</u> October 3, 1997.

prop up the ruble, but as Moscow cut the local currency free, it dropped like a rock and the country slipped further into recession.

Even worse, new regional products Global Investor Publishing designed to meet the needs of emerging market fund managers and financial institutions fell victim to a global recession. One of the most promising products, Brazil Portfolio, was dissolved in the wake of the devaluation of the local currency and systematic correction of the Brazilian economy after the production of only two issues.

From an operations standpoint, Global Investor Publishing was lean and efficient with four full time employees and a strategic vision to primarily use independent contractors in key countries to write and edit articles. This strategy enabled the company to leverage regional specific expertise maximizing utilization and minimize overseas fixed costs such as employee benefits and office administration.

Looking at the global markets falling into further disarray with no real turnaround in sight left both partners concerned about the young company's near future. After several long discussions on the condition of the current business and prospects for the future, they agreed that now was the time to make the necessary changes to ensure the company survived.

To reduce initial expenditures, all full time employees were laid off and in 1999, *Russia Portfolio* and *Central Europe Portfolio* were combined to form the new newsletter *Emerging Europe Portfolio*. Now the question of acquiring or merging with EMFR remained.

Dwight Ingalsbe

(Co-Founder, Marketing Director) – Mr. Ingalsbe has 12 years of international business to business publishing experience focusing on emerging markets information products. As co-founder of Global Investor Publishing, Inc., he has developed and managed the sales, marketing and publishing operations of the company. Mr. Ingalsbe's internet and technology experience includes electronic information marketing, web site design and management, and the development of electronic information databases. Mr. Ingalsbe previously founded a publishing consulting business that developed custom publishing products for firms involved in emerging markets. He launched the first magazine on the Russian construction industry and consulted on the re-launch of the Russian business and financial publication, Kommersant. Prior to that Mr. Ingalsbe worked for the Boston Business Journal, Johnston International Publishing and Institutional Investor with positions in advertising sales, marketing and production.

Brad Durham

(Co-Founder, Content Director) – Mr. Durham has 12 years of experience with emerging markets financial information and has been involved in the launch or early stage development of three separate media companies. As co-founder of Global Investor Publishing, Inc., he has jointly managed the business since it was founded in 1995. Mr. Durham was a financial editor and advisor to the Hearst Corporation in a publishing joint venture with the Russian newspaper publisher, Izvestia, and was an advisor and editor through the first year of Kommersant, now Russia's leading business newspaper. Prior to that, he was the managing editor of The WorldPaper, a 1.2 million circulation emerging markets business and finance publication. Mr. Durham's experience includes emerging markets financial content, managing editorial teams, and general business strategy. He has a law degree, a masters degree in journalism and is a regular contributor on emerging markets for several financial publications.

Emerging Market Funds Research, Inc.

In 1992, Ian Wilson established Emerging Market Funds Research (EMFR), a company specializing in financial data with particular attention focusing on emerging market funds. The company produces proprietary reports following the portfolio flows of equity and debt investment in and out of emerging market countries. But despite the company's early success, one of its largest and most important clients, Standard & Poor's, had decided not to renew its contract with EMFR. After this major blow to the company's financial performance, Ian began to wonder about the future of his young firm and whether or not its other clients such as Goldman Sachs, Morgan Stanley Dean Witter, and Merrill Lynch, could keep the company successful during the economic crisis spreading throughout the emerging markets. Making matters more difficult, Ian's resources were stretched pretty thin. Organizing the data for clients was consuming most of his time, making the marketing of the company's services to new clients a lower priority.

Global Investor Publishing – The Target Market

Durham and Ingalsbe saw their market as high net worth individuals and institutional investors who are either currently invested in emerging markets or are exploring investment into these markets and who use the internet to access information about investments. The market also includes the global community of market professionals including brokers, traders, analysts, sales personnel, investment bankers, and securities lawyers. These professionals serve investors both from major international capital markets and from inside the individual emerging markets.

Market Potential

Individual Investors **– Estimated Market: 27.6 Million Worldwide**

Individual investors, including online investors and high net worth individuals who are currently investing in emerging markets or are likely to do so in the near term.

Institutional Investors **– Estimated Market: 1 Million Worldwide**

Portfolio managers and advisors with dedicated and non-dedicated funds, pensions, managed accounts, trusts, etc., including buy-side analysts, who currently have exposure to emerging markets.

Market Professionals **– Estimated Market: 300,000 Worldwide**

Global and local market investment banks and brokerage firms, including traders, analysts, sales executives, strategists, and corporate finance personnel. Also included under this umbrella are consultants, law firms, stock exchanges and other market institutions, and government organizations involved in emerging markets.

Potential Advertising and Sponsorship Revenue

Fund Companies

Mutual fund and money management companies have an extensive budget for advertising and marketing of their products through direct sales techniques for no-load investing or through distribution channels such as brokerage houses. Money management firms such as Templeton, Scudder, T. Rowe Price, and Warburg Pincus Asset Management have emerging market fund products and are currently preparing their internet advertising strategies. In addition to U.S. based money management firms, managers of offshore funds and hedge funds have expressed interest in sponsoring a position on the site that would serve to market their funds while pre-qualifying investors.

Dedicated Emerging Market Funds: 2,500 Worldwide

International & Global Funds: 6,000 Worldwide

Domestic Funds in Emerging Markets: 17,000 Worldwide

Investment Advisors: 4,000

Investment Banks

Local Brokerage and Investment Banks: 700 Worldwide

International Investment Banks: 100 Worldwide

Stock Exchanges

Using mostly print medium, emerging market stock exchanges are active participants in international marketing. In addition, markets such as Turkey's Istanbul Stock Exchange, Brazil's Bovespa, and the

Warsaw Stock Exchange have built or are in the process of creating market web pages to increase their presence on the internet.

Online Trading Services

Of the top online trading services, several larger players have substantial advertising budgets, but have yet to tap and target investors interested or engaged in the emerging market areas. Present significant online trading services are E Trade, DLJ Direct, Datek, Ameritrade, Fidelity Powerstreet, Discover Brokerage, and Suretrade.

Online Financial Advertising Potential

Despite minor setbacks in the late 1990's, advertising revenue generated through the internet is expected to increase significantly over the next five years reaching $33 billion by 2004. Financial advertising revenue on content related websites from 1999 through 2002 is forecasted as follows:

Year	Revenue
1999	$200 million
2000	$280 million
2001	$380 million
2002	$500 million

The Decision

If Wilson were interested in a deal, the structure would be a key component to the transaction. Because EMFR was Wilson, he would be the obvious asset in the deal and the major driving factor behind the continued success of the fund data segment of the combined company. The only remaining question would be the actual structure of the transaction and the valuation.

John D. Sullivan, Ph.D.

Exhibit 1

Global Investor Publishing
Historical Financial Performance

Income	1998	1997	1996	1995
Subscription Revenue (newsletters)	306,694	354,461	192,697	57,392
Advertising Revenue	49,718	82,944	12,479	2,475
Content services (CSAM)	-	-	-	-
Consulting	28,450	-	-	-
EPFR - Data	-	-	-	-
Total Revenue	384,862	437,405	205,176	59,867
Cost of production and distribution	87,351	116,614	47,171	22,994
Gross profit	297,511	320,791	158,005	36,873
Operating Expenses				
Advertising & marketing	10,590	44,718	26,759	7,204
Bad debts	12,016	-	-	-
Bank service charges	3,517	4,070	1,123	457
Compensation to officers	57,600	-	-	-
Depreciation and amortization	111	2,059	1,021	320
Miscellaneous	-	6,923	2,352	5,336
Office expenses	71,628	37,131	16,903	10,898
Payroll taxes	12,757	3,851	-	-
Professional fees	5,611	5,369	3,030	9,793
Rent	12,174	9,686	-	-
Refunds	-	-	-	-
Salaries	74,466	32,453	-	-
Telephone	26,035	21,826	14,931	14,476
Travel & Entertainment	14,255	8,752	11,720	10,708
Total operating expenses	300,760	176,838	77,839	59,192
Operating Income	(3,249)	143,953	80,166	(22,319)
Other income	201	1,725	2,295	-
Legal fees	-	-	-	30,000
Interest expense	2,673	512	2,599	90
Net income before taxes	(5,721)	145,166	79,862	(22,409)
Income tax	456	456	456	456
NET INCOME	(6,177)	144,710	79,406	(22,865)

GIP Cost of Capital: 15%

Exhibit 2

Case Studies in Mergers & Acquisitions

Emerging Market Funds Research, Inc.

Historical Financial Performance

	1999	1998	1997	1996
Revenue				
Editorial service	44,972	70,693	61,829	63,614
Reports	59,300	63,771	90,592	80,768
Typesetting Service	5,250	11,500	11,500	9,250
Interest	5,160	1,973	347	-
Total Revenue	114,682	147,937	164,268	153,632
Expenses				
Advertising	556	-	-	672
Bank Charges	453	296	261	125
Books & Subscriptions	1,796	1,960	1,932	2,086
Conferences & Travel	139	-	1,021	1,316
Courier	51	212	552	760
Data	3,600	5,200	6,700	2,400
Depreciation	614	615	615	615
Income Taxes	-	-	12	-
Interest	1,346	195	59	-
Legal & professional fees	308	405	3,227	588
Management fees	87,500	119,000	128,838	128,843
Management health plan	2,867	5,138	4,983	4,219
Memberships	615	239	421	699
Office equipment	6,118	8,543	6,847	5,463
Office supplies	4,319	1,555	2,247	2,823
Storage	830	626	-	-
Telephone	2,480	4,265	4,528	2,932
Temporary help	792	25	1,375	310
Total Expenses	114,384	148,274	163,618	153,851
Net Income (loss)	298	(337)	650	(219)

John D. Sullivan, Ph.D.

Suggested Questions for Students

1. Is GIP's financial problems company or industry related?

2. Does the merger between GIP and Emerging Market Funds make sense?

3. How should the companies be integrated?

4. Is it critical that Wilson stay on board? If so, what role should he play?

Aetna 2000

Background

On March 1st, Aetna, the largest United States health insurer, announced an offer to purchase the company by WellPoint Health Networks and ING America Insurance Holdings in a deal worth $10 billion in cash and stock. Aetna's response to the offer was only that the company would evaluate the proposed transaction in conjunction with a comprehensive review of its present strategy and operations. Prior to the announcement, investors drove up the price of Aetna stock up 31 percent to 53 13/16.

Under the proposed transaction, ING America Insurance Holdings and WellPoint Health Networks would pay roughly $70 per share of Aetna stock. The purchase price would consist of $44 per share in cash and $26 in WellPoint common stock. ING America Insurance Holdings will act as an investment advisor to WellPoint.

Prior to the announcement of a potential merger, Aetna's stock price had floated near a 52 week low of 38 ½ per share on reporting of disappointing earnings in February, well below it's high of 99 7/8.

Aetna

Aetna Incorporated is a Connecticut company based in Hartford. Based on membership, the company is the largest health benefits company and one of the country's largest insurance and financial services organizations.

During the past several years, Aetna rapidly expanded its health operations through acquisitions and divested several other insurance businesses. In July of 1998, the company purchased New York Life Insurance Company's NYLCare health business. In October, Aetna then sold its interest in its individual life insurance business. By August of 1999, the company made another large investment by purchasing The

John D. Sullivan, Ph.D.

Prudential Insurance Company's health care business and in October, completed the sale of its Canadian operations.[1] Consolidated financial information can be found in exhibit 1.

As of the end of 1999, Aetna was divided into four areas:[2]

1. **Aetna U.S. Healthcare**: (exhibit 1)

   Health Products

       Health Maintenance Organizations

       Point of Service

       Preferred Provider Organization & Indemnity Products

   Group Life and Disability Insurance

   Long-Term Care Insurance

2. **Aetna Financial Services**: (exhibit 2)

   Financial Services Products

       Fixed & Variable Annuities

       Investment Advisory Services

       Financial Planning Services

       Pension Plan Advising

3. **Aetna International** (exhibit 3)

       Life Insurance

       Health Insurance

       Financial Services

---

[1] Aetna 1999 10K
[2] Aetna 1999 10K

4. **Large Case Pensions** (exhibit 4)

Retirement Products

In January 2000, Aetna announced a restructuring plan that would realign its business units. Under the plan, the company would group both the international and domestic health care within the same division under the name "Global Health." All financial services, including both international and domestic, would be grouped under "Global Financial." The strategy behind the plan was to enable Aetna to share its product expertise and technology between the domestic and international divisions.

As with most insurance companies offering "Managed Care" plans, Aetna is facing several outstanding lawsuits with regards to how it operates its HMO businesses. While a significant impact had yet to come, several states, as well as the federal government, were considering the implementation of an updated strict "patients bill of rights" that may adversely impact the financial operations of a health care company like Aetna.

WellPoint Health Networks

WellPoint Health Networks Inc. is one of the largest publicly traded managed health care companies with over 7.2 million medical members and approximately 30.6 million specialty members. The company offers a wide array of products in several markets including managed care services, underwriting, claims processing, actuarial services, medical cost management, and network access. WellPoint offers these main products, as well as others, to large and small employers, individuals, and seniors. In California, these products are marketed and sold under the name Blue Cross of California and outside California, they are marketed under Unicare. Financial Statistics for WellPoint are summarized in exhibits 7 through 9.

In July of 1998, WellPoint sold its Worker's Compensation Segment to Fremont Indemnity Company in a stock transaction worth $110.0 million. The sale of this segment allowed WellPoint to redirect its focus on national expansion of the health care market. Pursuing this strategy, the company purchased the Life and Health Benefits Management Division of Massachusetts Mutual Life Insurance Company and the Group Benefits Operations of John Hancock Mutual Life Insurance Company.

Corporate Issues

In July of 1998, WellPoint entered into an agreement to purchase the insurance company, Cerulean. Through its subsidiary Blue Cross and Blue Shield, Cerulean offered insurance products and administrative support for these products in the state of Georgia.

In September of 1998, policy holders of Blue Cross Blue Shield of Georgia filed a class action lawsuit regarding a conversion of Blue Cross and Blue Shield of Georgia from a "non profit" corporation to a "for profit" entity. The subsequent acquisition is pending and can be terminated by either party.

In September of 1999, the California legislature enacted into law a series of health care reform measures. Effective January 1, 2001, managed care entities must exercise ordinary care in the coverage of medical care requested by policy holders. Managed care organizations may be held liable if it fails to exercise "ordinary care" and the subscriber suffers substantial harm. Substantial harm may be defined as a loss of life, impairment of a limb or bodily function, disfigurement, severe and chronic pain, or significant financial loss. Similar legislative measures were enacted in Texas and have been discussed on the local, State, and Federal levels of government.

Competition in Health Care in the United States

As overall health care expenditures in the United States soar at an alarming rate, competition among health care providers and insurers have increased in an attempt to lower health care costs and maintain a steady revenue stream. Corporations, in order to lower "benefit expenditures" associated with providing health care coverage to employees, have placed an ever-increasing pressure on insurers to maintain or lower premiums. As a result, it is not unusual to find a company offering several health care plans to its employees. This increase in competition has forced health maintenance organizations like Aetna to focus their attention on health care expenditures attributed to their memberships utilization of their plan.

The critical component to increasing leverage in negotiating contracts with health care providers has been the number of participating members in any given area. Since hospitals are large fixed cost businesses, they primarily depend on volume to maintain solvency. By increasing members within a plan, health insurance companies can control volume and by doing so, significantly increase leverage in negotiating reimbursement contracts with health care providers.

But as health care providers increased their market share over the years, hospitals began to form groups and increase their leverage in key locations. One example of this is Partners Health Care in Boston. Formed in 1995 with the alignment of Massachusetts General Hospital and Brigham and Women's Hospital, over the past five years the organization has added six additional hospitals to the network significantly increasing their contract negotiating leverage with major health insurers in the area.

In late 2000, negotiations between Partners and a major health insurer, Tufts Health Plan, broke off when a contract could not be agreed upon. If unsettled, over a million Tufts Health Plan members would need to change plans or find a new Doctor within six months. A few weeks after the contract stalemate, Tufts and Partners came back to the bargaining table and agreed to the a new contract with price escalators for services. While both entities initially stood their ground, it was ultimately in both of their interests, as well as the participating members, to settle and compromise. These battles however, based on market share leverage, are likely to continue as pressure to control costs and maintain profitability increase.

Risks in Health Care in the United States

Risks in health care in the US come from several angles and each can have a material impact on both insurers and providers of health care. A "Patient's Bill of Rights," currently being discussed at both

John D. Sullivan, Ph.D.

the state and federal level, may shift a significant cost containment ability from the insurer to the patient. Other possible regulatory measures that might impact the industry would include adding an avenue to bring suit against an insurer if it can be proven that "adequate" care was not provided to the patient. While it has not been passed into law, this too could create a problem for insurers. Other regulatory risks may include, but will not be limited to, a prohibition of incentive plans for physicians designed to limit expenses, mandated coverage levels, increased reserve and capital requirements, changes to licensure or certification requirements, mandatory coverage of experimental procedures or drugs, anti-trust enforcement, mandatory access to specialists, and liabilities for negligent denials or delays in coverage.[3]

Another risk lies in the increased competition among health care insurers. Cost conscious customers may be more willing to leave more expensive coverage for lower premiums. Insurers, to maintain leverage with health care providers, will need a growing base of customers. This may be a difficult task given the ability of competition to continuously lower premiums to gain market share.

In this health care environment of rapid consolidation, Aetna will need to continue to uphold its success in the integration of other health care insurers.[4] Most acquisitions that fail do so for a variety of reasons. Some common possible reasons for acquisition under performance include: relying on unlikely synergies, paying too much, large variations in corporate culture, slow integration of the acquisition, poor due diligence, and a lack of corporate strategy.

---

[3] Aetna Inc. 1999 SEC Form 10-K405.

Exhibit 1

Aetna U.S. Healthcare
Operating Summary

	3 Months Ending September	
	1999	1998
(millions)		
Premiums	$4,935.8	$3,584.1
Net Investment Income	$163.8	$133.3
Fees & Other Income	$478.4	$381.9
Net Realized Capital Gains	($20.1)	$19.2
Total Revenue	$5,557.9	$4,118.5
Current & Future Benefits	$4,205.0	$3,084.5
Operating Expenses	$1,016.8	$725.6
Amortization	$108.6	$99.1
Total Benefits & Expenses	$5,330.4	$3,909.2
Income Before Tax	$227.5	$209.3
Income Tax	$100.1	$95.8
Net Income	$127.4	$113.5

John D. Sullivan, Ph.D.

Exhibit 2

Aetna Financial Services

Operating Summary

	3 Months Ending September	
	1999	1998
(millions)		
Premiums	$44.2	$38.6
Net Investment Income	$224.8	$278.2
Fees & Other Income	$134.2	$169.2
Net Realized Capital Gains	($11.2)	$1.9
Total Revenue	$392.0	$487.9
Current & Future Benefits	$201.1	$254.2
Operating Expenses	$93.0	$101.9
Amortization	$25.9	$36.2
Total Benefits & Expenses	$320.0	$392.3
Income Before Tax	$72.0	$95.6
Income Tax	$23.7	$29.0
Net Income	$48.3	$66.6

Case Studies in Mergers & Acquisitions

Exhibit 3

Aetna International

Operating Summary

	3 Months Ending September	
	1999	1998
(millions)		
Premiums	$562.0	$376.0
Net Investment Income	$117.0	$102.6
Fees & Other Income	$33.2	$35.4
Net Realized Capital Gains	$43.5	$1.2
Total Revenue	$755.7	$515.2
Current & Future Benefits	$487.9	$337.2
Operating Expenses	$145.6	$98.4
Amortization	$2.3	$2.4
Other	$28.5	$26.9
Total Benefits & Expenses	$664.3	$464.9
Income Before Tax	$91.4	$50.3
Income Tax	$69.3	$9.5
Net Income	$22.1	$40.8

Exhibit 4

Aetna Large Case Pensions
Operating Summary

	3 Months Ending September	
	1999	1998
(millions)		
Premiums	$32.8	$31.6
Net Investment Income	$241.1	$278.0
Fees & Other Income	$14.8	$8.9
Net Realized Capital Gains	($5.7)	($0.3)
Total Revenue	$283.0	$318.2
Current & Future Benefits	$248.0	$272.0
Operating Expenses	$7.5	$9.3
Amortization	$0.0	$0.0
Other	$0.0	($68.0)
Total Benefits & Expenses	$255.5	$213.3
Income Before Tax	$27.5	$104.9
Income Tax	$10.4	$40.7
Net Income	$17.1	$64.2

Exhibit 5

Aetna Consolidated Balance Sheets.

	As of December 31	
(Millions, except share data)	1999	1998
Assets:		
Investments:		
Debt securities available for sale, at fair value (amortized cost $29,409.4 and $30,730.1)	$28,661.60	$32,180.80
Equity securities, at fair value (cost $732.6 and $762.6)	$791.10	$800.50
Short-term investments	$788.20	$942.20
Mortgage loans	$3,238.20	$3,553.00
Real estate	$361.80	$270.30
Policy loans	$541.50	$458.70
Other	$1,394.80	$1,300.30
Total investments	$35,777.20	$39,505.80
Cash and cash equivalents	$2,504.50	$1,951.50
Short-term investments under securities loan agreement	$1,037.50	$753.60
Accrued investment income	$466.50	$537.10
Premiums due and other receivables	$2,751.10	$1,478.10
Reinsurance recoverable	$3,881.10	$3,897.20
Deferred income taxes	$352.00	$46.60
Deferred policy acquisition costs	$2,059.80	$1,768.60
Goodwill and other acquired intangible assets	$9,335.40	$9,143.50
Other assets	$1,341.70	$1,111.90
Separate Accounts assets	$53,332.20	$44,936.00
Total assets	$112,839.00	$105,129.90
Liabilities:		
Insurance liabilities:		
Future policy benefits	$17,599.30	$18,541.10

John D. Sullivan, Ph.D.

Unpaid claims	$4,976.50	$3,953.90
Unearned premiums 507.1 '28.9	$507.10	$428.90
Policyholders' funds left with the Company	$15,481.40	$17,632.50
Total insurance liabilities	$38,564.30	$40,556.40
Dividends payable to shareholders	$28.50	$35.20
Short-term debt	$1,887.70	$1,370.10
Long-term debt	$2,677.90	$2,214.50
Payables under securities loan agreement	$1,037.20	$753.60
Current income taxes	$307.60	$444.80
Other liabilities	$4,195.80	$3,007.00
Minority and participating policyholders' interests	$117.40	$148.40
Separate Accounts liabilities	$53,332.20	$44,936.00
Total liabilities	$102,148.60	$93,466.00
Aetna-obligated mandatory redeemable preferred securities of subsidiary limited		
liability company holding primarily debentures guaranteed by Aetna	-	$275.00
Commitments and contingent liabilities (Notes 3, 5 and 18)		
Shareholders' equity:		
Class C voting mandatory convertible preferred stock ($.01 par value, 15.000.000		
shares authorized, 11,61',816 issued and outstanding in 1998)	-	$862.10
Common stock ($.01 par value; 500,000,000 shares authorized; 142,680,694 in 1999 and		
141,272,628 in 1998 issued and outstanding)	$3,719.30	$3,292.40
Accumulated other comprehensive income (loss)	($655.60)	$177.80
Retained earnings	$7,626.70	$7,056.60
Total shareholders' equity	$10,690.40	$11,663.90
Total liabilities, redeemable preferred securities and shareholders' equity	$112,839.00	$105,129.90

Exhibit 6

Aetna CONSOLIDATED STATEMENTS OF
CASH FLOWS

(Millions)	1999	1998	1997
Cash Flows from Operating Activities:			
Net income	$716.90	$848.10	$901.10
Adjustments to reconcile net income to net cash provided by operating activities:			
Depreciation and amortization (including investment discounts and premiums)	$483.00	$451.40	$374.20
Gain related to sale of life business	-	($98.90)	-
Net realized capital gains	($71.90)	($271.80)	($334.20)
Changes in assets and liabilities:			
Decrease in accrued investment income	$63.00	$8.50	$46.00
Increase in premiums due and other receivables	($260.40)	($92.60)	($245.80)
Increase in deferred policy acquisition costs	($410.60)	($278.90)	($302.40)
(Increase) decrease in income taxes	($93.90)	($91.20)	$323.30
Net (increase) decrease in other assets and other liabilities	$245.00	($262.20)	($193.00)
Increase in other insurance liabilities	$969.60	$598.40	$656.40
Other, net	$28.40	($2.20)	$4.90
Net cash provided by operating activities	$1,669.10	$808.60	$1,230.50
Cash Flows from Investing Activities:			
Proceeds from sales and investment maturities of:			
Debt securities available for sale	$17,918.60	$20,254.60	$16,247.80
Equity securities	$588.60	$833.40	$961.40
Mortgage loans	$77.50	$90.40	$1,078.80
Real estate	$13.70	$136.50	$626.80
Other investments	$739.80	$639.10	$924.70
Short-term investments	$19,603.20	$21,229.10	$19,957.00
Life business	-	$1,000.00	-

John D. Sullivan, Ph.D.

Investment maturities and repayments of:			
Debt securities available for sale	$3,739.70	$2,849.40	$3,913.90
Mortgage loans	$485.60	$918.40	$1,726.50
Cost of investments in:			
Debt securities available for sale	($21,609.80)	($20,602.60)	($21,310.10)
Equity securities	($533.90)	($481.50)	($626.10)
Mortgage loans (480.3) (319.2) (255.3)	($480.30)	($319.20)	($255.30)
Real estate (58.8) (38.5) (66.8)	($58.80)	($38.50)	($66.80)
Other investments (812.5) (4,127.6) (1,033.5)	($812.50)	($4,127.60)	($1,033.50)
Short-term investments (18,924.8) (21,126.0) (20,291.7)	($18,924.80)	($21,126.00)	($20,291.70)
Acquisitions:			
NYLCare health care business	($48.80)	($1,080.60)	-
Prudential health care business	($512.50)	-	-
Other	($212.20)	($84.50)	($473.00)
Increase in property and equipment	($123.50)	($123.20)	($92.40)
Other, net	($9.40)	($97.40)	$83.00
Net cash (used for) provided by investing activities.	($159.80)	($130.20)	$1,371.00
Cash Flows from Financing Activities:			
Deposits and interest credited for investment contract.	$2,503.30	$2,046.40	$1,872.50
Withdrawals of investment contracts	($3,345.40)	($3,150.90)	($3,481.10)
Issuance of long-term debt	$2.00	$25.70	$4.70
Repayment of long-term debt	($33.30)	($153.00)	($34.30)
Net increase (decrease) in short-term debt	$519.40	$1,122.30	($46.70)
Common stock issued under benefit plans	$44.80	$39.60	$134.70
Common stock acquired	($512.50)	($394.90)	($523.10)
Redemption of mandatory convertible preferred stock	($275.00)	-	-
Dividends paid to shareholders	($153.50)	($170.90)	($174.90)
Other, net	$32.80	-	-
~ Net cash used for financing activities	($1,217.40)	($635.70)	($2,248.20)

Effect of exchange rate changes on cash and cash equivalents	($0.50)	($5.80)	($10.10)
Net increase in cash and cash equivalents	$291.40	$36.90	$343.20
Cash acquired from the NYLCare health business	-	$108.80	-
Cash acquired from the Prudential health business	$261.60	-	-
Cash and cash equivalents, beginning of year	$1,951.50	$1,805.80	$1,462.60
Cash and cash equivalents, end of year	$2,504.50	$1,951.50	$1,805.80

John D. Sullivan, Ph.D.

Exhibit 7

WellPoint Financial Statistics
As of April 2000

Share Price and Volume

52 Week Low	$48.25
Current Price	$71.81
52 Week High	$97.00
Beta	0.94
Daily Volume	407,100
Market Capitalization	4.45 Billion
Shares Outstanding	61.9 Million
Float	34.1 Million

Exhibit 8

WellPoint Financial Statistics

As of April 2000

Per Share Information

Book Value	$20.63
Earnings	$4.36
Sales	$109.34
Cash	$49.51
Price/Book	3.48
Price/Earnings	16.49
Price/Sales	0.66

Exhibit 9

WellPoint Financial Statistics
As of April 2000

Financial Summary

Sales	7.49 Billion
EBITDA	614.1 Million
Income Avail to Common	297.2 Million
Profit Margin	4.00%
Operating Margin	7.30%
ROA	6.69%
ROE	22.23%
Current Ratio	1.51
Debt/Equity	0.27
Total Cash	3.26 Billion

Case Studies in Mergers & Acquisitions

Suggested Questions for Students

1. How well positioned in the market is Aetna?

2. What would you consider is Aetna's strengths and weaknesses?

3. What is Aetna's most profitable segment and why?

4. Should Aetna be focusing on health care?

5. Why is Aetna the target of a takeover attempt?

6. Why might Aetna reject the offer?

7. Is the offer the right price for Aetna?

8. Would Aetna be better off merging with a large American health insurer?

9. If this is the case, why is this the only offer on the table?

10. Are Aetna's problems a result of the industry? Is WellPoint the right partner to solve these problems?

11. What is the correct price for Aetna?

12. Given the potential changes in the "regulations" of this industry, how would you value these potential issues?

13. What synergies does WellPoint bring to the table? Should these be used to value Aetna?

14. Should Aetna accept WellPoint's offer? If you were on the Board, how would you vote?

National Medical Care

In 1996, National Medical Care of Waltham, Massachusetts, a division of the conglomerate W.R. Grace and the largest dialysis service company in the United States, was put in play when the division President, Dr. Constantine Hampers, after a losing struggle to gain the role of W.R. Grace Chief Executive Officer, made an offer to purchase the division through a leveraged buyout for $4 billion in cash. The cash for the transaction would be raised primarily through an issue of debt and bank financing. Immediately following his offer, several competitive offers followed from competing dialysis service providers and manufacturers of dialysis products. While W.R. Grace immediately rejected Dr. Hampers' offer, the Board of Directors chose to evaluate the offers made by the dialysis product manufacturers Baxter International and Fresenius AG of Germany.

Background

End Stage Renal Disease or ESRD is characterized by the irreversible loss of kidney function requiring treatment with a synthetic kidney or a transplant to continue life. ESRD currently impacts the lives of more than 305,000 patients in the United States.[5] Incidence of kidney failure is increasing as a result of the aging population, diabetes, hypertension, glomerulonephritis, and cystic kidney disease. Nearly 80% of all patients with ESRD acquire the disease as a complication of one or more of these primary conditions.[6] Diabetes alone accounts for over 33% or 100,892 of the total ESRD patients with hypertension representing 24% or 72,961 patients. Obviously, any therapy advancements made in these disease areas could significantly slow the growth of this condition.

Based on information published by the Health Care Financing Administration (HCFA) of the Department of Health and Human Services, the number of patients in the US who received chronic dialysis

---

[5] United States Renal Data System: USRDS 1999 Renal Data Report. National Institutes of Health, National Institutes of Diabetes and Digestive and Kidney Disease. Bethesda, MD 1999 pp. 26
[6] Ibid

grew from approximately 66,000 in 1982 to approximately 214,103 by the end of 1996. This represents a compounded annual growth rate of 9%.[7] This annual growth rate may be attributed to a continuing growth of the general population, better treatment and survival of patients with hypertension, diabetes, and other illnesses that lead to ESRD. Moreover, improved technology has enabled older patients and those who could not tolerate dialysis due to other illnesses to benefit from this life sustaining treatment.

The End Stage Renal Disease program, almost entirely funded through the Federal government, has been a policy success story. "It has achieved the overriding goal established by Congress 20 years ago of financing expensive, lifesaving medical care for a highly vulnerable, very sick population."[8] Until the arrival of managed care, a program supported by the government and employers, the End Stage Renal Disease industry responded to Medicare budget cuts with efficiency, equipment technology, and expense adjustments. With the advent of managed care, however, the once abundant revenue stream service providers have been placed in jeopardy. A steady reduction in reimbursement from these third party payers combined with a Medicare program unwilling to increase reimbursement rates has made profitability for service providers a difficult task.

In 1993, the Federal government enacted the Omnibus Budget Reconciliation Act of 1993 (OBRA). Under OBRA, the Federal government amended the statutory ESRD Medicare Secondary Payor provisions affecting the coordination of benefits between Medicare and commercial health plans in the case of ESRD patients from the age of 65 and over who are eligible for Medicare and also covered by an employer health plan. This amendment lengthened the waiting period by three months effectively shifting an increasing amount of the cost to non-governmental third party payers.

A significant portion of dialysis service providers' revenue are derived from reimbursement provided by non-governmental third party payers. A substantial portion of third party health insurance in the United States is now furnished through some type of managed care plan, including health maintenance organizations (HMOs). Managed care plans are increasing their market share overall, and in the Medicare

---

[7] Ibid, pp. 39-56
[8] Iglehart, J.K. "The American Health Care System. The End Stage Renal Disease Program." The New England Journal of Medicine. Health Policy Report February 4, 1993., Vol. 328, No 5, p 366

population in particular. This trend may accelerate as a result of the merger and consolidation of providers and payers in the health care industry, as well as discussions among members of Medicare and Medicaid beneficiaries served through managed care plans.

Currently, there are only two types of treatment for ESRD: dialysis and kidney transplantation. Transplants are limited by the scarcity of compatible kidneys. Approximately 12,200 patients received kidney transplants in the United States during 1996.[9] Therefore, most patients must rely on dialysis, which is the process of removing toxins and excess water by artificial means. The primary types of treatment options for dialysis patients are hemodialysis and peritoneal dialysis and are based on the patient's medical conditions and needs.

According to HCFA, in 1996 there were approximately 3,082 Medicare certified ESRD treatment centers in the United States. Ownership of these centers was fragmented. As of 1996, the ten largest public and private providers of dialysis accounted for approximately 1,500 facilities (49% of the facilities) and cared for 108,000 patients (50% of the patient population). Privately owned freestanding clinics represented 27% of the facilities and hospital based clinics accounted for the remaining 23%.[10]

The dialysis industry had experienced significant consolidation in recent years. Large chains continued to purchase small to medium independent operators and chains. In 1994, National Medical Care, the largest provider of dialysis in the United States, acquired several dialysis centers for a total of $145.3 million in cash.[11] Over the next 12 months, National Medical Care increased their acquisitions, spending $260.8 million by the end of 1995. By contrast, the second largest provider of dialysis services, Vivra, spent only $4.3 million in dialysis related acquisitions in 1994.[12]

Small public companies have entered the dialysis market and have offered stock to acquisition targets, which has further accelerated the consolidation process. For example, in 1994, Renal Treatment

---

[9] United States Renal Data System: USRDS 1999 Renal Data Report. National Institutes of Health, National Institutes of Diabetes and Digestive and Kidney Disease. Bethesda, MD 1999 pp. 102-112
[10] Ibid, pp. 165-171
[11] W.R. Grace, 1994 Annual Report, p. 37
[12] Vivra, 1994 Annual Report, p. 17

John D. Sullivan, Ph.D.

Centers, purchased by Total Renal Care in 1998, spent $50.3 million in cash, issued 87,608 shares of common stock valued at approximately $1.8 million and issued a $7.5 million dollar note for seven acquisitions completed during the year. These acquired centers provided care to approximately 1,373 patients.[13] Income statements for two of NMC's larger competitors, Total Renal Care and Renal Care Group are summarized in exhibits 28 and 29.

Because of this increased consolidation, the availability of acquisition targets had decreased significantly. Part of the consolidation attractiveness to chains has been the ability to group additional facilities under a centralized management system. This centralized system allowed the provider to hold a tighter control over the expenses and operation of individual facilities. For example, billing may be conducted for several states through one location providing the dialysis chain with increased personnel cost savings. In the current reimbursement environment, consolidation by acquisition will continue to play a key role in the profitability and financial stability of many of the providers of dialysis care.

However, this does not mean that the corporate office dictates prescriptions for dialysis patients. Each facility conducted its operations, in large part, upon the applicable laws, rules and regulations of the jurisdiction in which the center was located. A patient's physician, either affiliated with the provider or a physician with staff privileges, has medical discretion as to the particular treatment modality and medications to be prescribed for the patient. Similarly, the attending physician had the authority to select particular medical products for each patient.

Acquisitions of these centers, primarily by larger chains or operators of smaller physician owed clinics, ranged widely with regards to purchase price. "Purchasing terms are usually based on potential revenue, i.e., number of regular patients in the facilities. Prices range from $10,000 to $40,000 per patient. During 1988-89, one hospital in Ohio bought a unit with 50 patients for $2.3 million, i.e., $46,000 per patient. The average purchase price in 1988, however was estimated at $18,000 to $20,000 per patient. Prices apparently fell in 1989 to an estimated range of $15,000 to $18,000 per patient; changes in federal

---
[13] Renal Treatment Centers, 1994 Annual Report, p. 14

income tax law, quite independent of ESRD, significantly slowed corporate acquisitions. In states without CON (Certificate of Need) regulations, the prices tend to be lower"[14] by as much as 15 to 20 percent.

WR Grace

In 1994, WR Grace was comprised of six separate divisions each operating as an individual profit center and generating $5.1 billion in total revenues and net income of $83 million. Of the six divisions, National Medical Care was the largest with $1.9 billion in revenues for 1994.

Grace Health Care - National Medical Care

National Medical Care or NMC, was established in 1972 by Dr. Constantine Hampers and was the largest provider of dialysis services in the United States with approximately 574 outpatient clinics and a patient base of 50,000 in 1995.[15] On a per patient basis, NMC held approximately 25% of the service market. But NMC had not grown so large without controversy. In 1995, The New York Times ran a series of articles on dialysis and specifically mentioned problems at National Medical Care as well as questionable business practices that could impact the quality of care for each patient. One such practice, known as "reuse," reduced the service providers medical supply cost significantly by reusing a patient's dialyzer several times with the same patient despite a warning label on each dialyzer that states "Single Use Only." While potentially inflammatory, research in dialysis has yet to prove reuse is harmful to patients undergoing treatment.

In 1995, NMC had sales of $2.077 billion, an increase of 10.75% over 1994 sales of $1.875 billion. Pretax operating income for this same period increased from $287 million in 1994 to $315 million in 1995.[16] National Medical Care financials are summarized in exhibits 4 through 12.

---

[14] Rettig, R.A., and Levinsky, N.G. <u>Kidney Failure and the Federal Government</u>, Committee for the Study of the Medicare End Stage Renal Disease Program, National Academy Press, 1991, pp. 130
[15] Wall Street Journal, February 5, 1996
[16] 1995 W.R. Grace Annual Report

Grace Packaging

With $1.4 billion in sales in 1994, Grace Packaging was the second largest operating division for the company. This division, specializing in advanced packaging for meat, poultry, cheese, and other perishable items, produces materials that preserve flavor and significantly extend the shelf life and appearance of packaged foods.

Grace Davidson

Grace Davidson produces fluid cracking catalysts that enhance crude oil creating motor fuels and other petroleum products. In addition, the division produces silica and zeolite absorbents that assist in the manufacturing process of paints, plastics, toothpaste, and other refining industries. In 1994, the division generated $610 million in revenue.

Grace Construction Products

Grace Construction Products are designed to strengthen concrete, fight corrosion, stop water damage, and protect structural steel against collapse in the event of fire. 1994 sales for construction products increased 16% from 1993 to $387 million.

Grace Dearborn

Grace Dearborn manufactures chemical products that enable customers to recycle process waters and render discharge water environmentally safe. 1994 sales for the division were $363 million.

Grace Container Products

With 1994 sales of $325 million, Grace sealants ensure the integrity of more than 400 billion cans and bottles each year making Grace Container Products the world leader in sealant technology.

The Bids

Both offers for the W.R. Grace Health Care division came from prominent worldwide dialysis product manufacturers with an eye towards an instant expansion of market share through this vertical merger. Prior to National Medical Care being put "in play" by Dr. Hampers, NMC purchased their products for clinics from Fresenius, Baxter, and to a much lesser extent, the small products division owned by NMC. By either Fresenius or Baxter purchasing the company, as important as the overnight increase in market share, was the strategic victory of keeping the competition from purchasing National Medical Care. Therefore, it became a crucial strategic deal for both dialysis product manufactures.

Baxter International Inc.

Baxter was currently the largest manufacturer of dialysis products worldwide holding 42% of the approximate 3.1 billion-dollar market. For 100% of the outstanding NMC stock, Baxter has offered $3.8 billion in stock and debt. Under the proposal, Baxter would include $1.8 billion in Baxter stock, extend W.R. Grace a note of $300 million, assume debt of $425 million, and make a cash payment to W.R. Grace of $1.275 billion. If the transaction were completed, Baxter would emerge as the largest integrated dialysis company in the world. Baxter's financial performance is summarized in exhibits 22 through 27.

Fresenius AG (Germany)

Fresenius AG was one of the largest manufacturers of dialysis products in the world with an estimated market share of 13%. (Exhibit 2) Fresenius owned and operated a few dialysis clinics in Europe and South America. Unlike Baxter, which has made an offer to purchase 100% of the outstanding stock, Fresenius has offered $2.3 billion for approximately 55.2% of NMC's stock. The remaining 44.8% of the outstanding stock would be held by existing W.R. Grace shareholders. Under this proposed transaction, Fresenius estimates 1996 new company sales of $3.5 billion and would become the largest fully serviced provider of dialysis in the world. The deal would be completely financed through an issue of debt primarily raised through banks. Fresenius' financials are summarized in exhibits 13 through 21.

Inside the Boardroom

The W.R. Grace Board of Directors needed to make a decision and the market was waiting. The Board had set its mind to selling the division, it was just a question of adequate price and fulfilling their obligations to their shareholders. During the Grace Board's deliberations, the Federal Government, through the Office of Inspector General, announced an investigation into the National Medical Care's billing practices with Medicare. While the Board had no idea of how large the potential liability of the investigation was, if any liability was warranted, it was widely rumored throughout the industry that a major public hospital chain was entertaining a partial settlement with the OIG for approximately $300 million. The Board continued to pursue the potential sale or partnership for its health care division.

Exhibit 1

Medicare's ESRD Spending

Hospital Admission	38.0%
Dialysis Treatment	28.5%
Drugs	10.5%
Physician Visits/Fees	10.5%
Lab	3.0%
Transportation	2.0%
Other	8.0%

Source: Health Care Financing Administration

John D. Sullivan, Ph.D.
Exhibit 2

Dialysis Products Market
Worldwide

Baxter	42.0%
Gambro	32.0%
Fresenius	13.0%
Other	13.0%

Source: Wall Street Journal 2/5/96

Exhibit 3

Market Comparison Between Service Providers

1994

	Revenue (Millions)	Pretax Profits (Millions)	Int'l & Domestic Clinics
NMC	$ 1,875.1	$ 227.1	624
Vivra	$ 284.0	$ 50.0	150
REN	$ 132.0	$ 14.0	60
RTC	$ 87.0	$ 12.0	46
TRC	$ 81.0	$ 11.0	65

Source: Company Filings

John D. Sullivan, Ph.D.
Exhibit 4

National Medical Care

Financial Snapshot

	1995	**1994**	**1993**
Revenue	$ 2,076.8	$ 1,875.1	$ 1,512.9
Income before Tax*	$ 104.6	$ 227.1	$ 192.0
Tax	$ 82.6	$ 102.4	$ 76.7
Net Income	$ 22.0	$ 124.7	$ 115.3

*Includes allocation of interest expense of 93.5, 60.4, and 43.9 for 1995, 1994, & 1993.

Source: 1995 W. R. Grace Annual Report

Exhibit 5

handwritten: current ratio = 1.25

National Medical Care

Net Assets as of Dec 1995

Current Assets	$ 665.9
Property & Equipment	399.3
Other Assets	993.7
Total Assets	2,058.9
Current Liabilities	533.8
Other Liabilities	89.8
Total Liabilities	623.6
Net Assets	1,435.3

Source: 1995 W.R. Grace Annual Report

John D. Sullivan, Ph.D.

Exhibit 6

NATIONAL MEDICAL CARE, INC.

NOTES TO COMBINED AND CONSOLIDATED FINANCIAL STATEMENTS--

Dollars in thousands

Note 18. Quarterly Summary (Unaudited)

	1st Qtr.	2nd Qtr.	3rd Qtr.	4th Qtr.
1994				
Net revenues	$ 401,899	$ 455,972	$ 490,152	$ 521,823
Cost of health care services and				
Medical supplies	244,972	267,045	274,113	287,327
Operating expenses	115,303	135,946	137,082	171,355
Interest expenses, net	3,446	3,249	3,290	6,120
Total expenses	363,721	406,240	414,485	464,802
Earnings before Income Taxes	38,177	49,732	75,667	57,021
Provision for Income Taxes	18,159	23,493	34,150	37,962
Net earnings	20,018	26,239	41,517	19,059
1993				
Net revenues	$ 338,560	$ 372,320	$ 393,297	$ 407,996
Cost of health care services and				
Medical supplies	201,982	213,286	235,862	239,734
Operating expenses	88,909	99,960	110,217	108,209
Interest expenses, net	3,181	3,535	1,943	3,054
Total expenses	294,072	316,781	348,022	350,997
Earnings before Income Taxes	44,488	55,539	45,275	56,999
Provision for Income Taxes	19,807	24,753	20,159	25,408
Net earnings	24,681	30,786	25,116	31,591

Exhibit 7

NATIONAL MEDICAL CARE, INC.

COMBINED AND CONSOLIDATED INTERIM STATEMENTS OF EARNINGS

(Unaudited)

(Dollars in thousands)

	Six Months Ended June 30,	
	1995	1994
NET REVENUES		
Health care services	$ 916,305	$ 730,793
Medical supplies	95,495	127,077
	1,011,800	857,870
EXPENSES		
Cost of health care services	516,929	444,203
Cost of medical supplies	64,106	67,814
General and administrative expenses	184,320	151,245
Provision for doubtful accounts	39,141	34,122
Depreciation and amortization	52,930	46,964
Research and development	3,594	3,155
Allocation of Grace expenses	19,940	15,763
Interest expenses, net, and related financing costs	11,660	6,695
Total	892,620	769,961
EARNINGS BEFORE INCOME TAXES	119,180	87,909
PROVISION FOR INCOME TAXES	53,079	41,652
NET EARNINGS	66,101	46,257

John D. Sullivan, Ph.D.

Exhibit 8

NATIONAL MEDICAL CARE, INC.
COMBINED AND CONSOLIDATED INTERIM BALANCE SHEET

(Unaudited)

(Dollars in thousands)

	June 30, 1995
ASSETS	
Current Assets:	
Cash and cash equivalents	$ 33,617
Accounts receivable, less allowance of $97,308	344,123
Inventories	100,147
Deferred income taxes	53,186
Other current Assets	66,417
Total Current Assets	597,490
Properties and equipment, net	361,648
Other Assets:	
Excess of cost over the fair value of net assets acquired and other intangible assets,	
Net of accumulated amortization of $232,249	836,650
Other assets and deferred charges	29,333
	865,983
Total Assets	1,825,121
LIABILITIES AND PARENT COMPANY INVESTMENT	
Current Liabilities:	
Current portion of long-term debt and capitalized lease obligations	83,117
Accounts payable	89,159
Accrued liabilities	220,856
Accrued income taxes	2,475
Total current liabilities	395,607

Long –term debt	11,851
Capitalized lease obligations	4,963
Deferred income taxes	71,595
Other liabilities	24,715
Total liabilities	508,731
Parent Company Investment:	
Parent Company Investment	1,313,743
Cumulative translation adjustment	2,647
Total Parent Company Investment	1,316,390
Total Liabilities and Parent	1,825,121

Handwritten notes:
- current ratio → 1.51
- QR → 1.26
- DSO → 2nd QTR → ~~237.80~~ 0.07 days
- debt ratio → 0.28

John D. Sullivan, Ph.D.

Exhibit 9

NATIONAL MEDICAL CARE, INC.
COMBINED AND CONSOLIDATED INTERIM STATEMENTS OF CASH FLOWS

(Unaudited)

(Dollars in Thousands)
Six Months Ended June 30,

	1995	1994
Cash Flows Provided by Operating Activities:		
Net earnings	$ 66,101	$ 46,257
Adjustments to reconcile net income to net cash provided by operating Activities:		
Depreciation and amortization	52,930	46,964
Provision of doubtful accounts	39,141	34,122
Provision for deferred income taxes	(6,389)	(8,937)
Loss on disposal of properties and equipment	1,829	1,702
Changes in operating assets and liabilities, net of effects of purchase Acquisitions and foreign exchange:		
Increase in accounts receivable	(61,541)	(77,435)
Increase in inventories	(5,294)	(5,922)
(Increase) decrease in other current assets	(12,711)	12,802
Decrease in accounts payable	(12,349)	(8,478)
(Decrease) increase in accrued income taxes	(17,031)	669
(Decrease) increase in accrued liabilities	(8,524)	11,416
Increase in other long-term liabilities	7,087	267
Increase in other assets and deferred charges	(863)	(9,065)
Other, net	(7,235)	(4,150)
Net cash provided by operating activities:	35,151	40,212

Cash Flows from Investing Activities:		
Capital expenditures	(47,648)	(41,209)
Payments of acquisitions, net of cash acquired	(64,764)	(173,900)
Payment of physician's contract agreements	(2,900)	
Other, net	2,701	288
Net cash used in investing activities	(112,611)	(214,821)
Cash Flows from Financing Activities:		
Advances from Parent, net	64,908	240,856
Proceeds on issuance of debt	9,813	2,343
Payments on debt and capitalized leases	(23)	(45,331)
Net cash provided by financing activities	74,698	197,868
Effects of changes in foreign exchange rates	(5,072)	1,060
(Decrease) increase in cash and cash equivalents	(7,834)	24,319
Cash and cash equivalents at beginning of period	41,451	24,084
Cash and cash equivalents at end of period	33,617	48,403

John D. Sullivan, Ph.D.
Exhibit 10

National Medical Care

Inventories

	June 30, 1995
Raw materials	$ 15,960
Manufactured goods in process	7,967
Manufactured and purchased inventory available for sale	33,955
	57,882
Health care supplies	42,265
Total	100,147

Exhibit 11

National Medical Care

NOTES TO COMBINED AND CONSOLIDATED INTERIM FINANCIAL STATEMENTS--
(Continued)

(Unaudited)

(Dollars in thousands)

Note 5. Quarterly Summary

	1st Qtr.	2nd Qtr.
1995		
Net revenues	$ 490,833	$ 520,967
Cost of health care services and medical supplies	284,432	296,603
Operating expenses	149,727	150,198
Interest expenses, net	5,807	5,853
Total expenses	439,966	452,654
Earnings before Income Taxes	50,867	68,313
Provision for Income Taxes	22,667	30,412
Net earnings	28,200	37,901
1994		
Net revenues	401,898	455,972
Cost of health care services and medical supplies	244,972	267,045
Operating expenses	115,303	135,946
Interest expenses, net	3,446	3,249
Total expenses	363,721	406,240
Earnings before Income Taxes	38,177	49,732
Provision for Income Taxes	18,159	23,493
Net earnings	20,018	26,239

John D. Sullivan, Ph.D.

Exhibit 12

National Medical Care

Net Revenues

(In millions)

	Years Ended December 31,			Six Months Ended June 30,	
	1994	1993	1992	1995	1994
DSD	$ 1,304	$ 1,206	$ 873	$ 721	$ 592
MPG	406	401	353	211	195
Homecare.	318	217	160	164	146
Intercompany Elimination's	(518)	(132)	(112)	(84)	(75)
Total Net Revenues	1,870	1,512	1,274	1,012	858

Net earnings

(In million)

	Years Ended December 31,			Six Months Ended June 30,	
	1994	1993	1992	1995	1994
Operating Earnings:					
DSD	$ 250	$ 192	$ 188	$ 135	$ 104
MPG	34	48	70	23	4
NMC Homecare	49	37	28	25	19
	333	277	286	183	127
Other Expenses:					
General Expenses, including					
Grace allocations	39	31	94	35	19
Research & Development,					

Including Grace allocations	29	32	29	17	13
Reduction in Carrying Amounts Of Assets to Estimated Fair Values	28		26		
Interest Expenses	16	12	11	12	7
Total Other Expenses	112	75	160	64	39
Earnings Before Income Taxes	221	202	126	119	88
Provision For Income Taxes	114	90	63	53	42
Net Earnings	107	112	63	66	46

John D. Sullivan, Ph.D.

Exhibit 13

Fresenius USA

Consolidated Balance Sheets

December 31, 1994 and 1993

(Dollars in thousands, except share amounts)

Assets	1994	1993
Current assets:		
Cash	$ 2,315	$ 5,552
Trade accounts receivable, less allowance for doubtful accounts of $1,744 in 1994 and $1,718 in 1993	42,671	39,992
Inventories, net	52,704	43,925
Prepaid expenses and other current assets	1,893	2,565
Total current assets	99,583	92,034
Property, plant and equipment, net	45,956	26,004
Intangible assets, net	39,498	40,821
Other assets	311	357
	$ 185,348	**$ 59,216**
Liabilities and Stockholders' Equity		
Current liabilities:		
Account payable	$ 13,128	$ 14,463
Account payable to affiliates, net	33,361	28,278
Accrued expenses	12,214	11,178
Short-term borrowings	22,330	14,425
Short-term borrowings from Fresenius AG	4,380	4,159

Current portion of long-term debt	8,356	2,182
Current portion of capital lease obligation	1,140	1,371
Income taxes payable	<u>95</u>	<u>453</u>
Total current liabilities	95,004	76,509
Long-term payable, less current portion	1,861	2,417
Note payable to FNA	274	274
Long-term debt, less current portion	25,963	40,358
Capital lease obligations, less current portion	<u>1,674</u>	<u>2,652</u>
Total liabilities	<u>124,776</u>	<u>122,210</u>

Stockholders' equity

Series preferred stock, authorized 600,000 shares, $1.00 par value, issued and outstanding 200,000 shares	200	200
Series F Common stock, authorized 40,000,000 shares, $.01 Par value, issued and outstanding 21,205,175 shares in 1994 and 17,636,700 shares in 1993	212	176
Capital in excess of par value	139,510	123,112
Currency translation adjustment	-94	-72
Accumulated deficit	<u>-79,256</u>	<u>-86,410</u>
Total stockholders' equity	60,572	37,006
	$ 185,348	**$ 159,216**

John D. Sullivan, Ph.D.

Exhibit 14

Fresenius USA

**Year ended
December 31.**

	1990	1991	1992	1993	1994
Statement of operations Data	(Dollars and shares in thousands, except per share data)				
Net sales	$ 76,996	$ 101,436	$ 128,607	$ 205,960	$ 254,344
Cost of sales	57,812	71,812	92,575	140,960	175,766
Gross profit	19,184	29,624	36,032	65,000	78,578
Selling, general and administrative and research and development	21,897	28,865	32,964	55,713	66,489
Litigation settlements	—	1,300	-400	—	—
Restructuring of operations	250	—	—	—	—
Operating income (loss)	-2,963	-541	3,468	9,287	12,089
Interest expense (net)	-1,109	-2,167	-2,447	-4,631	-4,195
Equity in earnings (loss) of Fresenius Brent	-8	84	70	86	—
Other income (expense), net	3	-191	-341	-149	-17
Income (loss) before income Taxes and extraordinary items	-4,077	-2,815	750	4,593	7,877
Income tax expense	-5	-15	-111	-900	-723
Income (loss) before extraordinary					

Items	-4,082	-2,830	639	3,693	7,154
Extraordinary items	—	255	—	—	—
Net income (loss)	$ (4,082)	$ (2,575)	$ 639	$ 3,693	$ 7,154

Net Income (Loss) Per Common Share

Income (loss) before extraordinary items	$ (0.26)	$ (0.18)	$ 0.03	$ 0.18	$ 0.31
Extraordinary items	—	0.02	—	—	—
Net Income (Loss) Per Common Share	$ (0.26)	$ 0.16)	$ 0.03	$ 0.18	$ 0.31

John D. Sullivan, Ph.D.
Exhibit 15

Fresenius Medical Care

Sources of Revenue

Year Ended December 31.

	1992		1993		1994	
	Total Revenues	Percent of Total	Total Revenues	Percent of Total	Total Revenues	Percent of Total
Hemodialysis	$ 92,349	72%	$ 134,117	65%	$ 170,579	67%
Peritoneal Dialysis	32,537	25	65,073	32	77,331	30
Other Products	3,721	3	6,770	3	6,434	3
Total	$ 128,607	100%	$ 205,960	100%	$ 54,344	100%

Exhibit 16

Fresenius USA

Cash Flow

Years ended December 31, 1994, 1993 and 1992

(Dollars in thousands, except share amounts)

	1994	1993	1992
Cash flow from operating activities:			
Net income	$ 7,154	$ 3,693	$ 639
Adjustments to reconcile net income to net cash provided by (used in) operating activities:			
Depreciation and amortization	8,772	6,893	3,619
Equity in earnings of Fresenius Brent	—	(86)	(70)
Gain on sale of fixed assets	(46)	(75)	—
Stock warrant issued to Fresenius AG as compensation for credit support	—	75	—
Other	—	—	(92)
Changes in assets and liabilities:			
Trade accounts receivable, net	(2,679)	(14,090)	(4,139)
Accounts receivable from affiliated companies, net	—	1,820	(325)
Inventories, net	(9,199)	(6,800)	(4,874)
Prepaid expenses and other current assets	672	(1,651)	269
Income tax receivable	—	56	47
Other assets	46	802	(730)
Account payable and accrued			

expenses	(299)	12,514	5,824
Income tax payable	(358)	453	–
Increase in net assets resulting from the acquisition of Fresenius Brent	____	782	____
Net cash provided by operating activities	4,063	4,386	168

Cash flow from investing activities:

Purchase of Abbott's renal dialysis business	–	(31,000)	–
Purchase of Critikon net assets	–	–	(500)
Expenditures for the direct costs of acquisition	–	(737)	–
Purchase of property, plant and equipment	(25,534)	(8,226)	(4,928)
Proceeds from sale of property, plant and equipment	46	128	55
Purchase of investments			(3)
Net cash used in investing activities	(25,488)	(39,835)	(5,366)

Exhibit 17

Fresenius USA

Inventories

As of December 31, inventories consisted of the following:

	1994	1993
Raw materials and purchased components	$ 3,071	20,094
Work in process	4,237	4,516
Finished goods	27,464	22,147
	54,772	46,757
Reserves	(2,068)	(2,832)
Inventories, net	$ 52,704	$ 43,925

John D. Sullivan, Ph.D.
Exhibit 18

Fresenius Medical Care

Facilities

Location	(approximate square feet)	Owned or Leases	Use
Walnut Creek, California	85,000	Leased	Corporate headquarters; warehousing; manufacture and assembly; and customer service.
Ogden, Utah	240,000	Owned	Production of disposable products.
Maumee, Ohio	26,000	leased	Production and warehousing of dialysate concentrate.

Exhibit 19

Fresenius Medical Care

Property, Plant and Equipment

As of December 31, property, plant and equipment consisted of the following:

	1994	1993
Land	$ 325	$ 325
Buildings and improvements	10,353	10,008
Machinery and equipment	14,596	11,828
Machinery, equipment and rental equipment under capitalized leases	11,429	11,163
Rental equipment	17,160	11,352
Leased equipment	2,353	646
Construction in progress	16,286	1,068
	72,502	46,390
Accumulated depreciation and amortization	(26,546)	(20,386)
Property, plant and equipment, net	$ 45,956	$ 26,004

John D. Sullivan, Ph.D.
Exhibit 20

Fresenius Medical Care

Intangible Assets

As of December 31, intangible assets consisted of the following:

	1994	1993
Goodwill	$ 0,789	$ 0,789
Manufacturing technology	15,629	15,629
Patents	3,427	3,427
Distribution rights	1,250	1,250
Other	2,927	2,019
	44,022	43,114
Accumulated amortization	(4,524)	(2,293)
Intangible assets, net	$ 39,498	$ 40,821

Exhibit 21

Fresenius USA

Long-term Debt

As of December 31, long-term debt consisted of the following:

	1994	1993
Term loan (a)	$ 5,000	$ 5,000
Note payable, discounted to present value (b)	8,731	10,629
10-1/2% convertible subordinated debentures, due 2002 [c]	—	1,155
10-1/2% convertible senior subordinated debentures, due 1997 [c]	—	381
Industrial revenue bonds (d)	—	5,200
Other	588	175
	34,319	42,540
Less current maturities	(8,356)	(2,182)
	$ 25,963	$ 40,358

John D. Sullivan, Ph.D.

Exhibit 22

Baxter International

YEARS ENDED DECEMBER 31 (IN MILLIONS, EXCEPT PER SHARE DATA)			1995
OPERATIONS	NET SALES		5,048
	Costs and expenses		
		Cost of goods sold	2,777
		Marketing and administrative expenses	1,084
		Research and development expenses	345
		Restructuring charges	103
		Special charge for litigation, net	96
		Allocated interest, net	96
		Goodwill amortization	28
		Other (income) expense	-5
	TOTAL COSTS AND EXPENSES		4,524
	Income (loss) from continuing operations		524
	Income tax expense		153
	INCOME (LOSS) FROM CONTINUING OPERATIONS		
	Discounted operations		
		Income (loss) from discounted operations, net of applicable income tax expense (benefit) of $88 in 1995, $52 in 1994 and $(181) in 1993	304
		Costs associated with effecting the business distribution, net of income tax benefit of $8	-26
	TOTAL DISCOUNTED OPERATIONS		278
	Income (loss) before cumulative effect of accounting changes		649
	Cumulative effect of change in accounting for:		

Case Studies in Mergers & Acquisitions

		Income Taxes	
		Other post employment benefits, net of income tax benefits of $7	
	NET INCOME		649
PER SHARE DATA	Earnings (loss) per common share		
	CONTINUING OPERATIONS		1.34
	Discontinued operations		
		Income (loss) from discounted operations	1.1
		Costs associated with effecting the business distribution	-0.09
	TOTAL DISCOUNTED OPERATIONS		1.01
	Cumulative effect of change in accounting for:		
		Income Taxes	
		Other post employment benefits	
	NET INCOME (LOSS)		2.35
	Average number of common shares and equivalents outstanding		277

John D. Sullivan, Ph.D.
Exhibit 23

Baxter International

NET SALES TRENDS BY MAJOR PRODUCT LINE

YEARS ENDED DECEMBER 31 (IN MILLIONS)	1995	1994	1993	Percent in 1995
Major Product Line	$	$	$	%
Renal	1,294	1,160	1,061	12%
Biotech	1,131	949	849	19%
Cardiovascular	730	632	562	16%
I.V. Systems/International Hospital	1,893	1,738	1,644	9%
TOTAL SALES	5,048	4,479	4,116	13%

Exhibit 24

Baxter International

NET SALES TREND BY GEOGRAPHIC REGION

YEARS ENDED DECEMBER 31 (IN MILIONS)	1995	1994	1993	Percent in 1995
Geographic regions	$	$	$	%
United States	2,492	2,292	2,112	9%
International	2,556	2,187	2,004	17%
TOTAL SALES	5,048	4,479	4,116	13%

John D. Sullivan, Ph.D.
Exhibit 25

Baxter International

YEARS ENDED DECEMBER 31 (IN MILIONS)	1995	1994	1993
	$	$	$
Capital expenditures	399	380	332
Acquisitions	44	60	107
Proceeds from asset dispositions	-91	-72	-5
Total investment transactions, net	352	368	434

Exhibit 26

Baxter International

INVENTORIES

AS OF DECEMBER 31 (IN MILLIONS)	1995	1994
	$	$
Raw materials	165	154
Work in Progress	164	136
Finished products	577	526
TOTAL INVENTORIES	906	816

John D. Sullivan, Ph.D.
Exhibit 27

Baxter International

PROPERTY, PLANT AND EQUIPMENT

AS OF DECEMBER 31 (IN MILLIONS)	1995 $	1994 $
Land	88	83
Buildings and leasehold improvements	701	663
Machinery and equipment	2,038	1,762
Equipment leased or rented to customers	341	348
Construction in progress	259	245
TOTAL PROPERTY, PLANT AND EQUIPMENT, AT COST	3,427	3,101
Accumulated depreciation and amortization	-1,678	-1,458
NET PROPERTY, PLANT AND EQUIPMENT	1,749	1,643

Exhibit 28

Competition Comparison

Total Renal Care, Inc.

INCOME STATEMENT DATA
Years ended May 31,

	1994	1,995
Net operating revenues	80,470	98,968
Facility operating Expenses	56,828	65,583
General and admin expenses	7,457	9,115
Provision for doubtful accts.	1,550	2,371
Depreciation and amortization	3,752	4,740
Total operating expenses	69,587	81,809
Operating income	10,883	17,159

John D. Sullivan, Ph.D.
Exhibit 29

Competition Comparison

Renal Care Group

	Year ended January 31	
	1994	1995
	$	$
Net Revenue	31,366	36,294
Operating costs and expenses:		
Patient care costs	24,255	28,357
General and Admin Exp.	1,129	930
Provision for doubtful acct	716	770
Deprecation and amortization	872	919
Total operating costs and exp.	26,972	30,976
Income from operations	4,394	5,318
Interest expense, net	185	183
Income before taxes	4,209	5,135
Provision for income taxes	1,074	944
Net Income	3,135	4,191

Suggested Questions for Students

1. How attractive is the merger potential to both Fresenius and Baxter?

2. How should the structure of the offers impact the decision of the W.R. Grace Board of Directors?

3. Why might a vertical acquisition shift the negotiation leverage to that of the seller?

4. How would you vote if you were a member of the W.R. Grace Board of Directors?

Teradyne

On August 2nd, 2001, Teradyne, Inc. (NYSE: TER) of Westford, Massachusetts announced that it would be acquiring GenRad, Inc. (NYSE: GEN), a leading manufacturer of automatic test equipment and related software. Under the terms of the definitive agreement, each share of GenRad stock would be converted into .1733 shares of Teradyne stock. At the close of the New York Stock Exchange on August 1st, Teradyne stock was valued at $35.10 effectively valuing the acquisition at roughly $260 million including an assumption of $85 million in debt. Teradyne believed that the acquisition would initially be dilutive, but expected through synergies and an increase in demand, would become accretive in 2002. Scheduled to close in the fourth quarter of 2001, the acquisition was dependant on GenRad shareholder and government regulator approval.

By September 2001, the economic condition of the United States had deteriorated. Accelerated by the terrorist attack on New York's World Trade Center Towers, American consumers further withdrew from traditional spending habits. During the month, Teradyne announced an unexpected third quarter loss of approximately $.32 per share. Previous analyst loss estimates were approximately $.11 per share. Amidst the economic turmoil and financial performance, the company began to eliminate 1,000 employees and reduced salaries of up to 15% for higher paid employees.[17]

Under the circumstances, the acquisition of GenRad may be in question. The board had to decide whether or not this was the right time to undertake such a complex integration and if the economy would recover in time to have the transaction contribute to earnings on schedule.

On the last trading day in September, Teradyne's stock closed at $19.50 and GenRad finished the month closing at $3.27 per share.

---

[17] "Teradyne Cuts 1,000 Jobs, Salaries, Confirms Forecast of Loss in Period." The Wall Street Journal. September 14, 2001.

John D. Sullivan, Ph.D.

Teradyne

Corporate Background

Teradyne manufactures automatic test equipment and related software for the electronics and communications industries. The company also is a leading manufacturer of connection systems used in the testing of electronic systems.

In December 2000, the company sold a controlling interest in its software testing business to an investor group. Teradyne remains a minority shareholder in the new company under the name Empirix.[18]

The products designed and sold by Teradyne are used in the design and testing of a large number of semiconductor products including logic, memory, mixed signal, and integrated circuits.

Electronic manufacturers who assist in the design, inspection, and testing of circuit boards and other electronic assemblies primarily use the company's circuit board test and inspection systems. Similar to semiconductor test systems, the circuit board test systems improve electronic product performance, increase product quality, shorten a manufacturers time to market, assist in manufacturing, minimize labor costs, and increase production yields.

The company also manufacturers broadband test systems used by the communications industry for Internet testing, customer service, and voice network maintenance.

Most of the company's test systems are complex and require support both from the customer as well as Teradyne. Pricing for these systems can reach $4 million or above. As of the year ending December 2000, no single customer accounted for more than 10% of the company's net revenue. The largest three customers accounted for 21% of revenue in 2000.

The distribution and sales of Teradyne's products are conducted both inside and outside the United States. While the company has sales offices throughout North America, it also maintains sales and service offices throughout South East Asia, Europe, Taiwan, Japan, and Korea. Almost all of the company's

---

[18] Teradyne, Inc. Securities and Exchange Form 10-K. December 31, 2000.

manufacturing is done in the United States, but a majority of the revenue comes from outside the U.S. International sales accounted for 54% of total revenue in 2000, 52% in 1999, and 46% in 1998.[19] Risk associated with international business tend to be country or region based and include political and economic instability, unfavorable trade policy, fund transfer problems, currency fluctuations, distribution, tax rates, and the ability to collect accounts receivable funds.

Teradyne has never paid a cash dividend and has maintained a policy to use earnings to finance expansion and growth.

Competition

Teradyne participates in a highly competitive environment that covers all of its business segments. Competitors are constantly improving products that may or may not be an improvement over Teradyne's products. It is therefore essential that the company continue to invest heavily in itself to further improve and create new products for the marketplace.

Employees & Corporate Headquarters

As of December 2000, Teradyne employed approximately 10,200 persons. The company has never experienced any labor problems and does not have any employees that are members of a collective bargaining group.[20]

Research and Development

For Teradyne to continue to compete in the marketplace, it needs to invest in both new product development and the improvement of its existing product base. In 2000, the company invested $300.9 million for new and existing products. Expenditures for research and development in 1999 and 1998 were

---

[19] Teradyne, Inc. Securities and Exchange Form 10-K. December 31, 2000
[20] Teradyne, Inc. Securities and Exchange Form 10-K. December 31, 2000

approximately $228.6 million and $195.2 million. Research and development accounted for approximately 10% of total net revenue in 2000, 13% in 1999, and 13% in 1998.[21]

Regulatory Issues

While the company has not experienced any significant costs associated with its compliance with numerous regulations designed to protect the environment, it cannot predict the future expenditures associated with regulatory compliance. Some of the environmental laws that impact the business include The Comprehensive Environmental Response, Compensation, and Liability Act, The Superfund Amendment and Reauthorization Act of 1986, The Occupational Safety and Health Act, The Clean Air Act, The Clean Water Act, The Resource Conservation and Recovery Act of 1976, and The Hazardous and Solid Waste Amendments of 1984.

GenRad

Corporate Background

GenRad, Inc. provides electronic manufacturing productivity solutions for contract and original equipment manufacturers of wireless and handheld devices, personal computers, business servers, DSL and other broadband switching and routing technologies, and other equipment devices used for the Internet and electronic commerce. While primarily located in the United States, GenRad also maintains facilities in Western Europe and Southeast Asia.

GenRad is organized into three business lines, each supported through its support and services division:

---

[21] Teradyne, Inc. Securities and Exchange Form 10-K. December 31, 2000

Process Solutions

The Process Solutions is based in Westford, Massachusetts and is comprised of seven lines of products primarily focusing on in-circuit test, x-ray test, and re-work solutions for electronic manufacturers. Products under this division range in price from $25,000 to $1,000,000.

Functional Solutions

Based in Westford, Massachusetts, the Functional Solutions division sells and markets functional test platforms for manufacturers of telecommunications, computers, and automobile electronics. Systems under this division typically sell for as little as $100,000 with a ceiling of approximately $500,000.

Diagnostic Solutions

GenRad, through its Manchester, UK facilities, provides customers with a wide array of diagnostic and information solutions tying design, manufacturing, and service into a single vision. This division accomplishes this goal through the its software and hardware solutions for the automotive and transportation customers, as well as other independent service providers.

Support and Services

Through its Support and Services Division, GenRad provides customers with on-site and remote support, maintenance programs, and programming and training to enable customers to optimize their GenRad hardware and software products.

John D. Sullivan, Ph.D.

Competition

GenRad participates in an intensely competitive industry. Competition from both domestic and foreign corporations exists across all business segments. Some of the competing companies are substantially larger than GenRad and have easier access to resources. Some of the company's principal competitors are Agilent Technologies, Teradyne Corporation, Siemans A.G., and Bosch. GenRad, in order to overcome its competition, targets customers' specific needs and carves out a niche rather than competes on a large, broad basis. The primary competitive factors are product performance, customer applications, engineering, customer support and service, and pricing. For GenRad to continue to compete in each of its product segments, research and development will play an ongoing critical component of the company's strategy.

GenRad sells and supports its products primarily through an in-house sales and service team. Currently the company maintains sales offices in the United States, Mexico, the United Kingdom, Germany, France, Switzerland, Italy, Sweden, the Netherlands, Singapore, and Malaysia. The company will also contract with independent companies throughout the world to provide sales and service support in areas not directly covered by GenRad's sales and support teams.

Employees & Corporate Headquarters

As of December 2000, GenRad employed 1,524 total employees including contracted employees. As a comparison, in the prior year, the company had 1,296 total employees. As of December 2000, no employee was a member of a collective bargaining agreement.[22]

---

[22] GenRad, Inc. Securities and Exchange Form 10-K. December 31, 2000

Customer Base

GenRad primarily targets and delivers products and services to original equipment manufacturers of electronics, electronic components and peripherals, contract electronics manufacturers, and transportation and automotive companies. While these industries make up the largest share of the company's sales, other smaller manufacturers are also focused on for future sales.

One of GenRad's primary customers is Ford Motor Company providing the automotive manufacturer with diagnostic equipment to assist Ford's dealers with the problem testing of electrical systems in Ford vehicles. At year-end December 2000, Ford accounted for approximately 22% of consolidated accounts receivable. For the years ending 1998, 1999, and 2000, the Ford business accounted for approximately 11%, 31%, and 20% of consolidated revenues.[23]

Research and Development

One of the keys to GenRad's continued success is the development of new products and the improvement of existing products on the market. Most expenditures in research and development are primarily associated with the hiring of staff and the improvements in software and hardware in all of the company's product segments. In 2000, the company spent approximately $29.0 million in research and development. Expenditures in 1999 and 1998 were $20.0 million and $19.0 million.[24]

Expansion through Acquisition

GenRad had expanded through the years, utilizing both same store growth and acquisition. In April 2000, the company purchased Autodiagnos AB, an automotive aftermarket diagnostic software and equipment vender based in Stockholm, Sweden with offices in England, the Netherlands, Germany, and the United States. For substantially all of the outstanding stock, GenRad paid $26.7 million in cash and

---

[23] GenRad, Inc. Securities and Exchange Form 10-K. December 31, 2000
[24] GenRad, Inc. Securities and Exchange Form 10-K. December 31, 2000

included the assumption of $6.0 million in debt. Legal and accounting expenditures for the transaction totaled $1.3 million.

Earlier in March 2000, the company acquired the assets of Nicolet Imaging Systems and the outstanding stock of Sierra Research Technology located in California and Massachusetts for approximately $40 million in cash. The transaction enabled the company to expand its x-ray inspection technologies and its repair/re-work equipment business.

In April 1998, GenRad purchased certain assets of the Manufacturing Execution Systems business of Valstar Systems Limited of Aberdeen, Scotland for $3.2 million in cash including approximately $0.2 million in acquisition costs.

Conclusion

With the stock market correction and the uncertainty of the immediate future of the United States and global economy, an acquisition of GenRad at this time may not seem appropriate. However, it may prove the key time to invest as interest rates continue to fall and stock prices remain suppressed. With the close looming in the near future, management had to decide on the fate of the deal before it was legally obligated to go through with the transaction.

Exhibit 1

GenRad, Inc.

CONSOLIDATED STATEMENTS OF OPERATIONS

YEARS ENDED DECEMBER 30, 2000, JANUARY 1, 2000 AND JANUARY 2, 1999

(in thousands, except per share amounts)

	2000	1999	1998
	$	$	$
Revenue:			
Products	275,480	232,362	159,290
Services	66,175	69,586	65,499
Total Revenue	341,655	301,948	224,789
Cost of revenue:			
Products	157,257	124,114	80,112
Services	46,694	42,643	38,775
Total Cost of Revenue	203,951	166,757	118,877
Gross margin	137,704	135,191	105,912
Operating Expenses:			
Selling, general and admin	80,723	63,216	67,890
Research and development	28,956	20,042	18,962
amortization of acquisition-related intangible assets	7,269	2,831	1,948
Acquired in-process research and development	500		10,097
Restructuring and other charges	1,291		8,753
Loss from impairment of intangible assets			4,906
Arbitration settlement			7,650
Total operating Expenses	118,739	86,089	120,206
Operating income (loss)	18,965	49,102	-14,294
Other income (expense)			
Interest income	196	212	399
Interest expense	-8,216	-1,374	-1,163
Other	165	-169	-541
Total other expense	855	-1131	-1,305

Income (loss) before income taxes	11,110	47,771	-15,599
Income tax benefit (provision)	10,537	-277	6,531
Net income (loss)	21,647	47,494	-9,068

Net income (loss) per share:

Basic	0,77	1,66	-0.32
Diluted	0,75	1,6	0

Weighted average shares outstanding:

Basic	28,205	28,669	28,003
Diluted	28,731	29,683	28,003

Exhibit 2

GenRad, Inc.

CONSOLIDATED BALANCE SHEETS
DECEMBER 30,200 AND JANUARY 1,2000

(IN THOUSANDS, EXCEPT PER SHAE AMOUNTS)

	2000 $	1999 $
Assets		
Current assets:		
Cash and equivalents	8,321	6,951
accounts receivable, less allowance of $828 and $ 1,487	114,355	81,276
Inventories	65,551	49,068
Deferred tax assets	12,781	
Other current assets	8,445	8,228
Total current assets	209,453	145,523
Property and equipment, net	47,620	43,194
Deferred tax assets	18,410	19,868
Intangible assets, net	91,497	38,686
Other assets	2,625	1,368
Total assets	3,699,605	248,639
Liabilities and Stockholders' Equity		
Current liabilities:		
Trade accounts payable	21,427	21,841
Accrued liabilities	11,779	5,921
Deferred revenue	10,185	9,388
Accrued compensation and employee benefits	10,645	6,750
Accrued income taxes	2,987	3,760
Current portion of long-term debt	48,590	2,353
Total current liabilities	105,613	50,013
Long-term liabilities:		
Long-term debt	45,050	3,653
Accrued pensions and benefits	8,999	9,175
Lease costs of excess facilities		3,922
Deferred revenue	1,232	1,005

Deferred tax liabilities	3,412	
Other long-term liabilities	4,542	4,036
Total long term liabilities	63,235	21,791
Total liabilities	168,848	71,804

Stockholders' Equity:

Common Stock	30,394	29,877
additional paid-in capital	225,738	221,854
Treasury stock	-31,292	-29,017
Accumulated deficit	-22,419	-44,066
Accumulated other comprehensive loss	-1,664	-1,813
Total stockholders' equity	200,757	176,835
Total liabilities and stockholders' equity	369,605	248,639

Exhibit 3

GenRad, Inc.

CONSOLIDATED STATEMENTS OF CASH FLOWS

YEARS ENDED DECEMBER 30, 2000, JANUARY 1, 2000 AND JANUARY 2, 1999

(in thousands)

	2000	1999	1998
Operating activities:	$	$	$
Net Income (loss)	21,647	47,494	-9,068
Adjustments			
Depreciation and amortization	25,544	14,928	15,312
Allowances for Acct rec. and inv.	8,260	-3,875	1,520
Stock-based compensation	551	590	639
(Gain) loss on disposal of prop. And eqp.	878	116	-281
Deferred income tax benefit	-11,975	-4,500	-7,500
Acquired in process research and development	500		10,097
Restructuring and other non-recurring charges	1,291		16,403
Loss from impairment of intangible assets			4,906
Increase (decrease) in operating assets and liabilities			
Account Receivables	-27,961	-17,386	10,257
Inventory	-17,338	-13,289	-4,120
Other Current Assets	605	-1,159	1,147
Account payable	-2,521	11,425	-2,951
Accrued liabilities	3,896	-10,400	-153
Deferred revenue	1,262	2,705	1,318
Accrued Compensation and employee benefits	-837	-1,602	-6,260
Other Current Assets	-1,327	-1,158	-2,335

Net cash provided by operating activities	2,745	23,889	28,931

Investing Activities:

Purchases of property and equipment	-18,255	-16,241	-15,157
Purchase of subsidiaries, net of cash acquired	-69,729	-490	-4,178
Development of intangible assets	-4,251	-4,886	-6,645
Net Cash used in investing activities	-92,235	-21,617	-25,980

Financing Activities:

Purchases from credit facility, net	87,534	-2,341	-2,433
Proceeds from employee stock plans	2,681	10,154	6,633
Purchase of treasury stock	-2,275	-18,716	-14,958
Net Cash provided by (used in) financing activities	87,940	-10,903	-10,758
Effects of exchange rates on cash	2,920	2,584	-1,078
Increase (decrease) in operating assets and liabilities			
Increase (decrease) in cash and equivalents	1,370	-6,047	-8,885
Cash and cash equivalents at beginning of the year	6,951	12,998	21,883
Cash and cash equivalents at end of the year	8,321	6,951	12,998

Exhibit 4

GenRad, Inc.

NOTES TO CONSOLIDATED FINANCIAL STATEMENTS
YEARS ENDED DECEMBER 30, 2000, JANUARY 1, 2000 AND JANUARY 2, 1999

	2000	1999
Inventories:	$	$
Raw materials	22,704	13,247
Work in process	31,378	17,891
Finished goods	11,469	17,930
	65,551	49,068
Other Current assets:		
Prepaid expenses	4,804	4,957
Other current assets	3,641	3,271
	8,445	8,228
Property and equipment:		
Leasehold improvements	14,376	13,738
Machinery and equipment	69,408	58,748
Service parts	17,381	12,459
	101,165	84,495
Accumulated depreciation	-53,545	-41,751
	47,620	43,194
Intangible Assets		
Goodwill	50,932	22,311
Capitalized and purchased Comp Software	15,486	11,244
Developed Technology	22,510	11,370
Assembled workforce	4,741	1,444
Other intangible assets	21,946	3,182
	115,615	49,551
Accumulated amortization	-24,118	-10,865
	91,497	38,686

John D. Sullivan, Ph.D.

Accrued pension and benefits:

Accrued U.S. pension	1,634	1,795
Accrued foreign pension	4,420	4,526
Accrued postretirement benefit	2,945	2,854
	8,999	9,175

Exhibit 5

Teradyne Inc.

ASSETS & LIABILITIES
DECEMBER 31, 2000 AND 1999

ASSETS	2000 $	1999 $
Current Assets		
Cash and eq.	242,421	181,345
Marketable Sec.	60,154	66,316
Acct. Rec.	420,040	296,159
Inventories:		
Parts	318,790	123,300
Assembled in process	159,123	145,393
Finished Goods	34,650	
	512,563	268,693
Deferred tax assets	93,958	49,716
Prepayments and other cur. Assets	48,698	45,458
Total current assets:	1,377,834	907,687
Property, plant, and equip.		
Land	54,774	41,774
Buildings and improvements	293,124	238,136
Machinery and equipment	831,159	692,383
Construction in progress	75,520	9,693
Total	1,254,957	981,986
Less: Accumulated Dep.	-521,171	-484,247
Net Property, plant and equipment	733,786	497,739
Marketable Securities	161,848	139,752
Other assets	82,400	23,035
Total assets	2,355,868	1,568,213

LIABILITIES

Current Liabilities:

Notes Payable	7,389	8,221
Current portion of long-term debt	169	4,659
Accounts Payable	153,897	104,335
Accrued Employees compensation	158,817	117,314
Deferred revenue and customer adv.	183,465	60,096
Other accrued liabilities	86,637	66,223
Accrued income taxes	28,914	31,478
Total current liabilities	619,288	392,326
Deferred tax liabilities	21,257	13,907
Long-term debt	8,352	8,948
Total liabilities	648,897	415,181

Exhibit 6

Teradyne Inc.

SHAREHOLDER'S EQUITY		
Common Stock (0.125$ par value)	21,570	21,290
Additional paid-in capital	334,241	234,198
Retained Earnings	1,351,160	879,544
Total Shareholder's equity	1,706,971	1,153,032
Total liabilities and shareholder's eq.	2,355,868	1,568,213

John D. Sullivan, Ph.D.

Exhibit 7

Teradyne Inc.

CONSOLIDATED STATEMENTS OF INCOME

	Years ended December 31,		
	2000	1999	1998
	(In thousands except per share amounts)		
	$	$	$
Net Sales			
Expenses			
Cost of sales	1,669,699	1,047,752	947,174
Engineering and development	300,920	228,570	195,158
Selling and admin.	362,562	256,392	212,885
	2,333,181	1,532,714	1,355,217
Income from operations	710,765	258,198	133,934
Interest and other income	30,724	17,307	13,514
Interest expense	-1,841	-1,656	-1,566
Income before income taxes	739,648	273,849	145,882
Provision for income taxes	221,894	82,155	43,765
Income before cumulative effect of chg. in acct pri.	517,754	191,694	102,117
Cumulative effect of chg. In acct. pri.	-64,138		
Net Income	453,616	191,694	102,117
Income per share before cumulative effect of chg., in acct pri.	2.99	1.12	0.61

Cumulative effect of chg. in acct.	-0.37		
Net Income per common share	2.62	1.12	0.61

John D. Sullivan, Ph.D.

Exhibit 8

Teradyne Inc.

CONSOLIDATED STATEMENTS OF CASH FLOWS

(In thousands)

		2000 $	1999 $	1998 $
Cash Flows from operating activities		453,616	191,694	102,117
	Net Income			
	Adjustments to reconcile net income to net cash			
	Deprecation	99,929	85,279	75,351
	Amortization	1,933	1,107	953
	Charge for excess inventory			23,000
	Deferred income tax benefit	-44,242	-4,101	-14,607
	Other non-cash income tax benefit	-10,997	4,354	-804
	Changes in operating assets and liabilities			
	Account rec.	-113,930	-76,856	81,630
	Inventories	-235,319	-2,346	-16,990
	Other assets	7,589	-24,576	-1,184
	Accounts Payable	226,798	115,750	-18,530
	Accrued income taxes	85,482	77,171	7,685
Net Cash provided by operating activities		470,859	367,476	238,621
Cash flows from investing activities:				
	Additions to prop, plant, and equipment	-235,189	-119,780	-119,457
	Increase in equipment manufacturing	-63,053	-31,376	-44,983

	Purchases of held to maturity marketable sec.	-409,180	-177,650	-20,000
	Maturities of held to maturity marketable sec.	394,006	118,990	20,000
	Purchases of available for sale marketable sec	-177,864	-204,824	-162,092
	Proceeds from sales and Maturities	177,104	169,824	224,951
	Cash acquired in acquisition	1,885		
Net Cash used by investing activities		-312,291	-244,816	-101,581

Cash flows from financing activities:

	Payments of long-term debt	-5,283	-1,333	-1,615
	Issuance of common stock under stock option	55,263	82,323	26,579
	Acquisition of treasury stock	-147,472	-207,819	-51,158
Net cash used by financing activities		-97,492	-126,829	-26,194
Increase(decrease) in cash and cash equ.		61,076	-4,169	110,846
		181,345	185,514	74,668
Cash and cash eqi. At the end of the year		242,421	181,345	185,514

John D. Sullivan, Ph.D.

Suggested Questions for Students

1. Given the state of the US economy, is this the right time for this merger?

2. If the merger has been calculated as dilutive in the first year, how has the stock market impacted the valuation and financial performance of the transaction?

3. What are the synergies that Teradyne is betting on? How much risk is associated with these cost reduction forecasts?

Trans World Airlines

Background

In 1995, Trans World Airlines, buckling under the capital demands of the airline industry and competition, had filed for Chapter 11 Bankruptcy protection. During this time, the company had taken significant steps to correct its financial problems and improve its operating efficiencies with limited success. By February 2001, two groups had announced their intention to purchase the struggling airline. The first group, under the name Jet Acquisitions Group of Scottsdale, Arizona, comprised of airline industry experts and investors, had offered $889 million for TWA without any further details, but had stated that they wanted the company to remain an independent airline. The second bidder, American Airlines, had offered $500 million in cash for substantially all of the assets of TWA including their hub operations in St. Louis and most of the company's real estate leases and maintenance bases at more than 60 airports. Under this offer to the bankruptcy court, American would further assume Trans World Airline's liabilities including worker's compensation, employee post retirement benefits, most of TWA's aircraft leases which represented approximately $3.5 billion in commitments, and to allow the company's frequent flyer program to convert to American's "AA Advantage Program" mile for mile. Ultimately, under this scenario, either bid would need the initial approval of the bankruptcy court Judge before moving forward for regulatory approval.

The Company

Trans World Airlines, a Delaware Corporation formed in 1978 with headquarters in St. Louis, Missouri, was originally created in 1934 as Transcontinental & Western Air. Serving 23.9 million passengers in 1998, TWA is the eighth largest United States airline and regularly flies to 93 cities throughout the US, Mexico, Europe, the Middle East, Canada, and the Caribbean using 185 aircraft.[25]

---

[25] Trans World Airlines. Securities and Exchange Form 10K. 1998.

The company's route structure is principally organized into two distinct sections: North America and International. The North American route system flies passengers and cargo to 36 states, Puerto Rico, Mexico, Canada, and the Caribbean. As of December 1998, the North American passenger revenue accounted for 88.5% of total revenue compared to 85.9% during 1997.[26]

In North America, TWA operates a hub and spoke structure using Lambert International Airport in St. Louis as its major domestic hub. In St. Louis, TWA held approximately 76% market share (not including commuter flights) with 357 scheduled daily flights serving 78 cities, with the next closest competitor holding only 13%.[27]

Trans World Airline's second major hub, New York's JFK, provides service to 27 domestic and international cities with approximately 40 daily departures. JFK is the largest international gateway from North America. The use of both Lambert and JFK is structured so the airline can easily support both its North American and International connecting flights.

The company's international routes provide passengers with both nonstop and connecting flights from both New York and St. Louis with the majority of TWA's transatlantic flights being scheduled out of JFK. The present system is designed to feed domestic service to international cities. As of 1998, TWA carried passengers through JFK to Barcelona, Cairo, Lisbon, Madrid, Riyadh, Rome, and Tel Aviv. International flights from St. Louis were limited to London's Gatwick Airport. In 1997, the company dropped several international routes that financially under performed including New York to Frankfurt, New York to Athens, Boston to Paris, and non-stop service from JFK to several domestic cities.

Fleet Modernization

TWA presently operates in a highly competitive and capital-intensive industry where slight movements in passenger volume or revenue can have a significant impact on financial results. One problem experienced by many airlines is the operational performance of its aircraft. As part of its ongoing corporate

[26] Trans World Airlines. Securities and Exchange Form 10K. 1998.
[27] Trans World Airlines. Securities and Exchange Form 10K. 1998.

strategy, TWA has created a fleet modernization plan to improve cost savings through less maintenance, aircraft operating efficiencies, and two pilot aircraft. The plan is also designed to simplify the company's fleet structure in order to decrease maintenance costs and crew training. Despite the initial capital costs of acquiring or leasing new aircraft, TWA believes the benefit through cost savings, economies of scale, and crew training will offset the short-term capital outlays in the long run. In addition, to comply with the Airport Noise and Capacity act of 1990, the company will need to filter out its aircraft to comply with the new regulations.

Since 1996, the company had achieved several goals. The first goal was to reduce the average age of its fleet from 19.0 years at the end of 1996 to 16.2 years by the end of 1998. During this time, the company also improved its reliability through on time performance.[28]

By the end of 1996, the company had retired 14 B-747s and 11 L 1011s heavy aircraft. Within fourteen months of this move, all the remaining B-747 and L 1011 aircraft had been phased out of service.

To fill the gaps left by the retiring aircraft, the company had entered into several contracts to purchase new aircraft. Since 1996, TWA has ordered a total of 27 B-757 aircraft and as of 1998, taken delivery of 16. The remaining B-757 aircraft are scheduled for delivery in 1999 and 2000. In 1998, the company also took delivery of two B-767-300ER aircraft with an additional plane due in 1999.

The company has also ordered 39 new MD-83 aircraft and as of 1998, taken delivery of 13. The remaining aircraft will be delivered in 1999.

In 1998, TWA had announced that it had planned to acquire an additional 125 new aircraft including 50 Boeing 717-200 for delivery in 2000, 50 Airbus A318 for delivery in 2003, and 25 Airbus A320 for 2008.

By restructuring its fleet, TWA has significantly shifted the type of aircraft operated to narrow-body aircraft from wide-body aircraft. In 1996, the ratio of narrow to wide body was 80%/20% with an

---

[28] Trans World Airlines. Securities and Exchange Form 10K. 1998.

average seat per plane of 161. By 1998, the ration of narrow to wide body was 91%/9% with an average seat per plane of 137. Given the upcoming deliveries in 1999, the company expects the ratio to slightly shift to 92%/8% and increase the average seat per plane to 145 and ultimately decrease the age of the fleet to approximately 11.3 years.

Employee Base

At the end of 1998, Trans World Airlines employed 21,261 full time equivalent employees. A large number of these employees were union belonging to either the International Association of Machinists and Aerospace Workers (IAM), the Airline Pilots Association (ALPA), and the Independent Federation of Flight Attendants (IFFA).

In 1994, the company renegotiated its contracts with each of the unions and eliminated certain raises for 1994 and 1995 with the exception of a 1% semi-annual raise beginning in 1995. Non-union and management had made similar concessions.

Cost Containment

In addition to the large capital costs associated with aircraft, each airline is also subjected to the possibility of large swings in fuel prices. TWA utilizes more than 20 separate suppliers for jet fuel and has contracts with several of these suppliers. The terms of these contracts vary depending on each supplier and generally include agreements in price, payment terms, and quantities for a specified period of time.
The company will also purchase additional fuel if the price and availability are in the best interests of TWA. From time to time, the company will also trade fuel and store jet fuel in facilities in key locations. In 1998, the company began entering into future jet fuel price swaps for a small percent of its 1999 projected fuel requirements.

But despite TWA's hedging strategies and fuel storage capabilities, the cost of fuel is still driven by crude oil prices. Production and refinement, as well as choices in the types of fuel produced may have a significant impact on the availability of fuel for air travel. As a result, regardless of hedging techniques, fuel costs could materially impact the financial performance of the airline. In 1996, aircraft fuel prices increased significantly with only a moderate decline in 1997. While fuel costs declined again in 1998, 1999 reflected higher fuel prices and depending on the company's fuel consumption, may further negatively impact the financial results of the company. Fuel usage and cost is summarized in Exhibit 1.

Competition

When the United States federal government passed the Airline Deregulation Act of 1978, the airline industry instantly engaged in fierce competition. Low-cost low fare rates were the marketing strategies of several "no frills" new airlines entering the industry straining older mature airlines with higher operating costs. To remain financially competitive, several airlines merged and also formed alliances with international carriers to increase service across the globe.

Frequent flier mileage plans, ground service, and other in-flight services emerged to attract customers and maintain or grow market share. But despite several attempts by airline management to increase revenues and cut operating expenses, intense price competition had forced several airline companies into Chapter 11 bankruptcy protection with no hope of re-emerging.

Trans World Airlines competes in both the domestic and international markets. In the domestic United States market, entrance into the airline industry, from a regulatory standpoint, is fairly easy and existing carriers may enter or exit a particular route without regulatory approval. As a result, many of TWA's routes may quickly shift from high to low competition in a relatively short period of time and vice versa.

The level of competition in the international market generally depends on the individual country of destination and any agreements the United States may gave with a specific foreign government. Unlike domestic fares, international fares ultimately fall under the Department of Trade, but most airlines do retain some discretion in determining appropriate ticket prices.

John D. Sullivan, Ph.D.

Regulatory Issues

Slot Restrictions

Airports such as JFK, LaGuardia, Chicago O'Hare, and Ronald Reagan Washington, have been deemed as high traffic and as a result, have limited slots available for takeoff and landing during peek hours.

Noise Abatements

The Noise Act required airlines to reduce noise levels in commercial aircraft with specific compliance deadlines. Companies such as TWA had two basic options under this Act. The first was to retrofit older aircraft, categorized as Stage 2 aircraft, with new quieter equipment. The second option would be to replace older Stage 2 aircraft with modern Stage 3 aircraft. By 1994, each airline was to phase out or retrofit 25% of their Stage 2 aircraft and by 1996, 50% of their Stage 2 aircraft. By 1999, 100% of the fleet must meet Stage 3 requirements. To comply with the 1996 requirement, TWA retrofitted DC-9 aircraft with engine hushkits at a cost of approximately $55.5 million.

Labor

Under the Railway Labor Act, the right of airline employees was established to organize and bargain collectively. The Railway Labor Act provides detailed procedures to be followed before a lawful work stoppage can occur. TWA has collective bargaining agreements with four domestic unions that represent 85% of the company's workforce.

Aging Aircraft

In 1990, the FAA initiated several directives mandating changes to maintenance programs for older aircraft. Each plane must undergo extensive structural modifications before a designated number of flights or deadlines set in 1994. Most of TWA's fleet currently falls under these directives.

Safety

All airlines fall under the safety regulations set forth by the Federal Aviation Administration. The FAA monitors aircraft maintenance and operations including equipment, training, communications, and anything else the FAA deems a safety issue. For the administration to ensure the company's compliance with safety regulations, TWA is required to obtain operating, airworthiness and other certificates before operations can begin.

In addition, the company must comply with safety regulations in the transportation of cargo and any public health policies initiated at both the federal and state levels.

Foreign Ownership of Shares

Under the Federal Aviation Act of 1958, non-U.S. citizens may not own more than a 25% voting stake in a United States airline.

Environmental

Each airline operating in the United States must comply with several environmental regulations including The Clean Air Act, the Clean Water Act, the Comprehensive Environmental Response Compensation and Liability Act of 1980 and the Resource Conservation Recovery Act. At the state level, other environmental regulations, depending on the state and location in the state, may also include other agencies such as sewer disposal that would regulate TWA. The company believes they are currently operating in compliance with all environmental regulations.

John D. Sullivan, Ph.D.

Legal Proceedings

On July 17, 1996, TWA Flight 800 crashed shortly after takeoff from New York in route to Paris, France. Of the 230 passengers and flight crew, there were no survivors aboard the Boeing 747 aircraft. Currently, the airline is a defendant in several lawsuits relating to the crash. The company believes its current insurance coverage is sufficient to cover the liability from the suits. However, it is difficult to ascertain the damage the crash has caused in so far as a decrease in revenues caused by public perception of the incident.

Conclusion

Under TWA's present operating structure, it seemed like a difficult task for the airline to re-emerge from bankruptcy protection with a healthy financial condition. The options, given the required enormous future capital investment, were fairly limited. Either TWA could find a suitor acceptable to the Bankruptcy Court or face the growing possibility of a complete liquidation.

Exhibit 1

Trans World Airlines

Fuel Consumption and Cost

	1998	Year End 1997	1996
Gallons Consumed (in millions)	675.8	730.3	838.9
Total Cost (in millions)	$344.6	$480.9	$585.2
Average Cost per Gallon	$0.51	$0.66	$0.70
Percent of Operating Expenses	10.4%	14.3%	15.6%

John D. Sullivan, Ph.D.

Exhibit 2

Trans World Airlines

Statement of Income

Three Months Ended September

	2000	*1999*
Operating Revenue		
Passenger	$881,918	792,166
Freight and mail	$24,399	$23,030
All other	$66,386	$61,230
TOTAL	$972,702	$876,426
Operating Expenses:		
Salaries, Wages & benefits	$336,424	$327,300
Costs associated with contract		$33,515
Aircraft fuel and oil	$170,947	$112,026
Passenger sales commissions	$32,359	$49,366
Aircraft maintenance materials and repairs	$34,853	$38,478
Depreciation and amortization	$32,104	$34,245
Aircraft rent	$141,272	$112,030
Other rent and landing fees	$48,357	$51,910
All other	$187,360	$176,485
TOTAL	$983,676	$935,355
Operating loss	($10,973)	($58,929)
Other Charges (Credit):		
Interest expense	$20,410	$22,399
Interest & investment income	($3,252)	($4,310)
Disposition of assets, gains & losses-net	($1,041)	($1,031)

Other charges & credits-net	($17,510)	($21,741)
TOTAL	($1,393)	($4,683)
Loss before income taxes	($9,580)	($54,246)
Provision (credit) for income taxes	($25,203)	($556)
Loss before extraordinary items	($34,783)	($53,690)
Extraordinary items		
Cumulative effect of accounting change		
Net loss	($34,783)	($53,690)
Preferred stock dividend requirements	$3,515	$5,864
Loss applicable to common shares	($38,298)	($59,554)

John D. Sullivan, Ph.D.
Exhibit 3

Trans World Airlines

Statement of Income

Nine Months Ended September

	2000	*1999*
Operating Revenue		
Passenger	$2,479,541	$2,264,791
Freight and mail	$73,999	$72,354
All other	$183,082	$169,862
TOTAL	$2,736,622	$2,507,007
Operating Expenses:		
Salaries, Wages & benefits	$998,436	$944,209
Costs associated with contract		$37,768
Aircraft fuel and oil	$456,272	$276,620
Passenger sales commissions	$100,407	$144,799
Aircraft maintenance materials and repairs	$89,867	$111,385
Depreciation and amortization	$97,439	$106,529
Aircraft rent	$411,494	$300,695
Other rent and landing fees	$145,821	$148,667
All other	$536,479	$514,480
TOTAL	$983,676	$2,585,152
Operating loss	($99,593)	($78,145)
Other Charges (Credit):		
Interest expense	$67,121	$71,810
Interest & investment income	($8,392)	($12,222)

Disposition of assets, gains & losses-net	($3,885)	$716
Other charges & credits-net	($53,201)	($58,408)
TOTAL	$1,643	$1,896
Loss before income taxes	($101,236)	($80,041)
Provision (credit) for income taxes	$1,051	$550
Loss before extraordinary items	($102,287)	($80,591)
Extraordinary items		($866)
Cumulative effect of accounting change	($12,844)	
Net loss	($115,131)	($81,457)
Preferred stock dividend requirements	$10,563	$17,590
Loss applicable to common shares	($125,694)	($99,047)

John D. Sullivan, Ph.D.

Exhibit 4

Trans World Airlines

Balance Sheets

Assets

	Sep. 30, 2000	Dec. 31, 1999
Current assets:		
Cash and cash equivalents	$157,062	$180,443
Receivables	254,732	155,070
Spare parts, materials & supplies	106,333	101,179
Prepaid expenses & other	79,958	53,197
TOTAL	589,085	489,889
Property:		
Property owned:		
Flight equipment	339,864	443,710
Prepayments on flight equipment	69,034	45,810
Land, buildings and improvements	79,277	77,021
Other property and equipment	90,383	90,115
Total property owned	578,558	646,656
Less accumulated depreciation	179,033	161,153
Property owned-net	399,525	485,503
Property held under capital leases:		
Flight equipment	176,094	176,094
Land, building and improvements	52,355	50,321
Other property held under capital leases	8,598	7,096
Total property held under capital leases	237,047	233,511
Less accumulated amortization	147,944	127,845
Property held under capital leases-net	89,103	105,666

Total property-net	448,628	591,169
Investments & other assets:		
Investments in affiliated companies	90,276	82,901
Investments, receivables and other	139,692	133,973
Routes, gates and slots-net	170,427	181,983
Reorganization value in excess	625,802	657,267
TOTAL	1,026,197	1,056,124
Grand Total	$2,103,910	$2,137,182

John D. Sullivan, Ph.D.

Exhibit 5

Trans World Airlines

Balance Sheets

Liabilities & Shareholder Equity

	Sep. 30, 2000	**Dec. 31, 1999**
Current liabilities:		
Current long-term debt	$175,164	$67,080
Current obligations under capital leases	39,814	38,664
Advanced ticket sales	304,647	198,722
Accounts payable, principally trade	340,333	263,624
Accounts payable to affiliated companies	5,203	6,250
Accrued expenses:		
Employee compensation and vacations earned	122,228	149,701
Contributions to retirement and pension trusts	22,918	15,165
Interest on debt and capital leases	13,466	14,235
Taxes	11,438	12,111
Other accrued expenses	199,375	195,340
Total accrued expenses	369,485	386,552
TOTAL	1,234,646	960,892
Long-time liabilities and deferred credits:		
Long-term debt	416,495	600,909
Capital lease	98,055	127,143
Postretirement benefits	509,334	502,097
Noncurrent pension liabilities	16,984	17,572
Other	109,171	99,479
TOTAL	1,150,039	1,347,200

Shareholder's Equity	803	723
Additional paid in capital	733,224	728,038
Accumulated deficit	(1,014,802)	(899,671)
TOTAL	(280,775)	(170,910)
Grand Total	$2,103,910	$2,137,182

John D. Sullivan, Ph.D.

Suggested Questions for Students

1. How did TWA weaken its financial strength?

2. What financial burdens are on the horizon for TWA? Can they retrofit jets? If so, how much does it cost on average to retrofit? (the DC-9 can be used as an estimate here)

3. Did TWA flight 800 impact their business in the long term?

4. How competitive is the airline industry?

5. Is TWA competitive? What are they doing right? What do they need to improve?

6. How would you value the TWA?

7. Can the airline emerge from bankruptcy protection on its own?

8. Aside from cash, what are the benefits to the Jet Acquisition Group?

9. What are the drawbacks to this group? What are their capital resources like? Is this a one shot deal to turn TWA around?

10. How is the bid from American Airlines different?

11. What are the benefits to a merger between American and TWA?

12. Do you see any potential anti-trust issues with the combination of American and TWA?

13. If TWA ultimately failed, would this impact air travel in the United States? If it would, should the United States government bail the airline out?

14. Are there any potential drawbacks to such a merger?

Should the bankruptcy court judge seek out potential offers by other large airlines? Are there any potential drawbacks to this strategy?

The Proposed Merger of Hewlett Packard and Compaq Computer

On September 4, 2001, Hewlett-Packard Company (NYSE: HWP) and Compaq Computer Corporation (NYSE: CPQ) announced to the markets a merger agreement that would create a new technology giant worth at the time combined $87 billion dollars. Under the terms of the proposed transaction, the deal was expected to close in 2002 and Compaq shareholders would receive 0.6325 of a newly issued HP share for each share of Compaq owned valuing Compaq at approximately $25 billion. The merger was expected to be accretive adding to Earnings Per Share in its first fiscal year of operation (2003).

Once the transaction is completed, HP shareholders would own approximately 64% of the new company and Compaq shareholders would hold the remaining 36%. Under U.S. federal income tax law, the transaction would most likely be tax free for both sets of shareholders.

The new company would be organized under four operating units: Printing and Imaging, Access Devices, IT Infrastructure, and Services. The new company will have a leading market position in each of these areas, as well as storage and management software. The merger is expected to generate synergies that achieve savings of $2.5 billion annually and further improve an existing cost structure.

At best, the stock market reaction to the merger was mixed. Within six weeks of the merger announcement, Walter Hewlett, the son of Hewlett-Packard co-founder William Hewlett, hired the proxy solicitation firm MacKenzie Partners, possibly signaling the potential fight between the firm's merger plans and the Hewlett family. The Hewlett family trust owns approximately 5% of Hewlett-Packard's outstanding common stock and could deliver a significant blow to the merger plans set in motion in early September.

Following the Hewlett family public concerns over the merger, The David and Lucille Packard Foundation announced on December 7, that it too would oppose the transaction. The market reacted swiftly to the news. As a result of the simple opposition to the deal by the Packard Foundation, Compaq shares dropped 13% closing at $9.70. The Packard Foundation holds approximately 10% of HP shares. Including all heirs to Hewlett-Packard the families own roughly 19% of the company.

Analysts following the merger and subsequent negative news were skeptical of whether or not the transaction could be completed. Most analysts suggested that for the deal to be approved, nearly 70% of the current Hewlett-Packard institutional shareholders would need to support the merger.

Despite the setbacks, HP and Compaq management continued to go forward with the merger plans seeking approval from the European Commission and the Federal Trade Commission in the United States.

Hewlett-Packard announced that it would continue to meet with investors, customers, and employees to educate them on the benefits of the transaction. While the deal may look in jeopardy to the market, management of both HP and Compaq believed it would succeed.

Background

Hewlett-Packard Company

In 1939, HP was formed through a partnership between William R. Hewlett and David Packard. Later, in 1947, the firm was incorporated under the laws of the State of California. In 1998, the company shifted strategy and moved the state of incorporation from California to Delaware.

The company's business strategy is divided into two approaches. The first is to compete against other narrowly focused companies in the industry in both products and services within the servers, software, storage, services and support, PCs, workstations, personal information appliances, and printers and supplies markets.[29]

The second approach the company takes in its strategy is to leverage the depth of its products and services across all of its business segments.

---

[29] Hewlett-Packard Company. Securities and Exchange Form 10-K. October 31, 2000.

At the end of 2000, HP was divided into three primary business segments:

Imaging and Printing Systems

Computing Systems

IT Services

Imaging and Printing Systems

Under the Imaging and Printing Systems business unit, the company designs and manufacturers laser and inkjet printers, scanners, personal color copiers and faxes, digital senders, wide and large format printers, print servers, work management software, networking solutions, digital photography products, imaging and printing supplies, imaging and software solutions, and image related professional and consulting services.

Computing Systems

Under the Computing Systems business segment, the company provides a wide variety of computer systems for commercial and consumer markets including PCs, PC servers, laptops, workstations, and software and storage solutions.

IT Services

The IT Services segment offers consulting, education, design and installation services, as well as ongoing support and maintenance, mission critical support and problem solving, and outsourcing and utility computing services. Under this division, financing arrangements for products range from leasing, automatic upgrade services, general financing, and venture financing.

International Operations

Hewlett-Packard is a large global company that draws approximately half of its revenue from overseas. During the last three years three fourths of this revenue were generated in Europe and the Far East with a majority of revenue coming from customers rather than governments.

Product Life Cycles

In any technology business, the ability to respond quickly to changes in the market poses a significant challenge to any company. Because many of HP's products have a relatively short product life cycle, it is critical that the company ensures smooth transitions from current products to new products with as few delays as possible. Any delay carries the possibility of a material impact on both future revenue and earnings.

Research and Development

Hewlett-Packard Laboratories provides the leading arm of the research team together with each of the three-business segment's individual research teams. Because research and development of new and better products is critical to the future of the company, HP allocated $2.6 billion in fiscal 2000, or 5.4% of net revenue, to research and development. As a comparison, in the two previous years, the company spent $2.4 billion each year that represented 5.8% of revenue in 1999 and 6.0% in 1998.

Employee Base

As of fiscal year end 2000, Hewlett Packard employed approximately 88,500 persons worldwide.

Compaq Computer Corporation

Founded in 1982 and based in Houston, Texas, Compaq Computer Corporation designs and manufactures hardware, software, solutions and services, enterprise computer solutions, fault tolerant and business critical solutions, communication products, and desktop and portable computers.

The company owns or leases various business, sales, service, research and development, warehouse, and manufacturing offices and facilities in over 500 cities in 58 countries. The key manufacturing facilities in the United States are located in California and Texas. Outside the domestic corridor, the company uses manufacturing facilities in Scotland and Brazil. Customer service centers are located throughout the world with the largest in Massachusetts, Georgia, Texas, and Ireland.

Compaq is primarily organized into four business segments. The first, Enterprise Computing, designs, enhances, and manufactures advanced computer and telecommunication products such as business critical servers and industry standard servers. This business unit accounted for approximately 34% of Compaq's consolidated revenue in 2000.

The second business segment, Compaq Global Services, generated approximately 16% of total revenue in 2000. This segment delivers infrastructure and solution design implementation, management, and support services to corporations and customers. Warranty coverage is provided through Compaq customer service area, as well as some outside resellers and independent service companies.

The third business segment, Commercial Personal Computing, provides commercial use computing through workstations, desktops, portable computers, monitors, internet access equipment, and life cycle management products. This business segment produced for approximately 31% of the company's total revenue in 2000.

The last segment, Consumer, targets customers that use computers almost entirely for home use. This segment is targeted directly and offers Internet ready desktop and laptop products through a network of retailers. The Consumer division accounted for approximately 18% of Compaq's consolidated sales.

John D. Sullivan, Ph.D.

Acquisition Strategy

In early 2000, Compaq purchased the configuration and distribution assets of InaCom Corporation for approximately $370 million in cash and assumed liabilities. After the merger, Compaq created Custom Edge Incorporated, a wholly owned subsidiary that would operate the business acquired by InaCom.

In August 1999, Compaq divested an 81.5% equity interest in AltaVista to CMGI Incorporated for CMGI stock valued at $1.8 billion. The equity stake in AltaVista was included in the purchase of Digital Equipment Corporation.

In February 1999, the company purchased Shopping.com for $257 million. For accounting purposes, the transaction was considered an acquisition.

The company has maintained an active acquisition strategy over the past few years. In 1998, Compaq purchased Digital Equipment Corporation for $9.1 billion. Through a large global network, Digital was an industry leader in implementing and supporting networked business solutions.

International Operations

Compaq is a global corporation that operates in more than 200 countries. International operations are organized in North America, Asia-Pacific, Japan, Latin America, China, and Europe, the Middle East, and Africa. Each region is responsible for sales and marketing within their own area. Compaq's revenue generated 55% of its revenue outside the United States and 36% of the company's revenue was derived from Europe, the Middle East, and Africa. Most of the remaining international revenue came from Japan, Asia-Pacific, and Latin America.

Manufacturing

Compaq utilizes two methods to manufacture products. The first, building products to demand, maximizes manufacturing efficiencies by producing large volumes of basic product configurations.

Case Studies in Mergers & Acquisitions

The second approach, configuring products to order, configures products to meet the hardware and software needs of customers. Both manufacturing methods are designed for ultimate efficiency and utilize "just in time" manufacturing, inventory management, and distribution.

Research and Development

To improve existing products and develop new and exciting technology, Compaq has continued to invest in itself. In 2000 and 1999, the company invested $1.5 billion and $1.7 billion in research and development.[30]

Employee Base

At year-end 2000, Compaq employed approximately 70,100 full time employees and 24,500 temporary or contract persons.

Competition

Most sections of the computer industry are intensely competitive with American and international companies fighting for market share. One key characteristic of this market is the pressure to develop and introduce new and better hardware and software products. To survive, a company must compete on distribution capability, product and service performance, product quality and price, marketing, and brand name.

The Economic Cycles and Impact on Technology

Economic conditions have a general correlation to sales and profits in the technology industry. During times of economic expansion, as were found in most of the 1990s, consumers and corporations tend spend more on upgrading existing computer systems or expanding technology for a growing workforce.

---

[30] Compaq Computer Corporation. Securities and Exchange Form 10K. December 31, 2000.

Conversely, in times of economic recession, technology spending drops significantly as corporations and consumers try to get by on what they have already in place. In the last recession in the United States that started in the late 1980s and extended into the early 1990s, several large computer corporations that were either over extended or failed to have the right product, failed to survive through the rough times never realizing the prosperity that followed.

In the fall of 2001, economists in the United States after much debate declared the economy in recession. After one of the largest economic expansions in US history, the country had fallen to meet the same fate as Europe and Japan.

Responding to the Internet crash of 1999 and 2000 and the terrorist attack on the World Trade Center, the Federal Reserve Bank lowered interest rates to record lows in 2001 with little or no positive response from corporate or consumers. Over the months that followed, economic indicators like Consumer Confidence, Consumer Spending, Manufacturing, Industrial Manufacturing, Retail Sales, and Unemployment also didn't look promising extinguishing the possibility of a turnaround in early 2002.

The Decision

Management at HP and Compaq were in a precarious position. While both teams believed in the merits of the acquisition, the markets were responding negatively with the founding families publicly fighting the transaction through a proxy fight. To complicate matters, the United States had followed the rest of the world into economic recession pulling down the profitability of the technology industry. While some economists argued that there was little doubt as to whether the economy would turn around by early or mid 2002, others believed the recession could merely be at the beginning meaning the United States was in for the long haul. With that in mind, the argument that the merger would add to earnings by its close in 2003 might prove a difficult goal for the new company.

Exhibit 1

Top 5 Institutional Holders of HP	% of Shares Outstanding
Capital Research & Management	3.5%
Barclays Global Investors	2.8%
Banc of America Capital Management	2.8%
State Street Global Advisors	2.3%
State Farm Insurance Companies	2.1%
Total	13.7%

John D. Sullivan, Ph.D.
Exhibit 2

Corporate Stock Performance

Compaq Computer Corporation

	2000		1999	
	High	Low	High	Low
Q1	$33.00	$24.69	$49.25	$30.13
Q2	$30.25	$24.50	$31.56	$21.19
Q3	$31.42	$25.00	$28.00	$22.25
Q4	$14.70	$14.70	$28.75	$18.69

Month End	2001
Jan	$23.57
Feb	$20.08
Mar	$18.11
Apr	$17.41
May	$15.91
Jun	$15.27
July	$14.89
Aug	$12.31
Sept	$8.31
Oct	$8.75
Nov	$10.15

Case Studies in Mergers & Acquisitions

Exhibit 3

Corporate Stock Performance

Hewlett Packard

Month End	2001	Month End	2000
Jan	$47.50	Jan	$23.12
Feb	$51.62	Feb	$26.27
Mar	$46.06	Mar	$30.59
Apr	$50.97	Apr	$30.90
May	$39.34	May	$36.83
Jun	$30.66	Jun	$36.97
July	$31.00	July	$31.64
Aug	$30.48	Aug	$36.60
Sept	$26.03	Sept	$35.80
Oct	$30.25	Oct	$31.15
Nov	$28.17	Nov	$29.62
		Dec	$43.59

Month End	1999
Jan	$17.07
Feb	$15.92
Mar	$22.14
Apr	$25.13
May	$22.81
Jun	$23.12
July	$25.01
Aug	$27.04
Sept	$24.83
Oct	$23.36
Nov	$22.26
Dec	$21.40

John D. Sullivan, Ph.D.

Exhibit 4

Hewlett Packard Company

Financial Performance by Business Segment

Imaging and Printing Systems

Years Ended October 31, (in millions)

	2000	1999	1998
Revenue	$20,476	$18,550	16,709
Earnings from Operations	$2,746	$2,335	$2,043

Computing Systems

Years Ended October 31, (in millions)

	2000	1999	1998
Revenue	$21,095	$17,814	17,315
Earnings from Operations	$960	$850	$480

IT Services

	Years Ended October 31,		
	(in millions		
	2000	1999	1998
Revenue	$7,129	$6,255	$5,685
Earnings from Operations	$634	$575	$748

John D. Sullivan, Ph.D.

Exhibit 5

Hewlett Packard Company

For the Years Ending October 31

(in millions)

	2000	1999	1998
Net revenue:			
Products	41,446	36,015	33,585
Services	7,336	6,355	5,834
Total net revenue	48,782	42,370	39,419
Costs and expenses:			
Cost of products sold	29,727	25,305	24,044
Cost of services	5,137	4,415	3,746
Research and development	2,646	2,440	2,380
SGA	7,383	6,522	5,850
Total costs and expenses	44,893	38,682	36,020
Earnings from operations	3,889	3,688	3,399
Interest income and order, net	993	708	530
Interest expense	257	202	235
Earnings from continuing operations before taxes	4,625	4,194	3,694
Provision for taxes	1,064	1,090	1,016
Net earnings from continuing operations	3,561	3,104	2,678

Exhibit 6

Hewlett Packard Company

Assets

(in millions)

Assets

	2000	1999
Current assets:		
Cash and cash equivalents	3,415	5,411
Short-term investments	592	179
Accounts receivable, net	6,394	5,958
Financing receivables, net	2,174	1,889
Inventory	5,699	4,863
Other current assets	4,970	3,342
Total current assets	23,244	21,642
Property, plant and equipment, net	4,500	4,333
Long-term investments and other assets	6,265	5,789
Net assets of discontinued operations		3,533
Total assets	34,009	35,297

Case Studies in Mergers & Acquisitions

John D. Sullivan, Ph.D.
Exhibit 7

Hewlett Packard Company

Liabilities and Shareholder Equity

(in millions)

Liabilities and stockholders' equity

	2000	1999
Current liabilities:		
Notes payable	1,555	3,105
Accounts payable	5,049	3,517
Employee compensation	1,584	1,287
Taxes	2,046	2,152
Deferred revenues	1,759	1,437
Others	3,204	2,823
Total current liabilities	15,197	14,321
Long-term debt	3,402	1,764
Others	1,201	917
Stockholders' equity		
Common stock	19	20
Retained earnings	14,097	18,275
Other income	93	
Total stockholders' equity	14,209	18,295
Total liabilities and stockholders' equity	34,009	35,297

Exhibit 8

Case Studies in Mergers & Acquisitions

Hewlett Packard Company

Inventory

	2000	1999
Finished goods	4,251	3,581
Purchased parts and fabricated assemblies	1,448	1,282
	5,699	4,863

John D. Sullivan, Ph.D.
Exhibit 9

Compaq Computer Corporation

Income Statement

(in millions)

	2000	1999	1998	1997	1996
Statement of Income:					
Net revenue:					
Products	35,667	31,902	27,372	24,122	19,611
Services	6,716	6,623	3,797	462	398
Total net revenue	42,383	38,525	31,169	24,584	20,009
Costs and sales:					
Products	27,624	25,263	21,383	17,500	14,565
Services	4,793	4,535	2,597	333	290
Total costs and sales	32,417	29,798	23,980	17,833	14,855
SGA	6,044	6,341	4,978	2,947	2,507
Research and development	1,469	1,660	1,353	817	695
Restructuring	-86	868	393		52
In-process technology			3,196	208	
Other expense, net	1,664	-1076	-69	21	17
	9,091	7,793	9,851	3,993	3,271
Income (loss) before income taxes	875	934	-2662	2,758	1,883

Exhibit 10

Compaq Computer Corporation

Assets

(in millions)

Assets

	2000	1999
Current assets:		
Cash and cash equivalents	2,569	2,666
Short-term investments		636
Trade accounts receivable, net	6,715	5,622
Leases and other accounts receivable	1,677	1,063
Inventories	2,161	2,008
Other assets	1,989	1,854
Total current assets	15,111	13,849
Property, plant and equipment, net	3,431	3,249
Other assets, net	6,314	10,179
Total Assets	24,856	27,277

John D. Sullivan, Ph.D.
Exhibit 11

Compaq Computer Corporation

Liabilities and Shareholder Equity

(in millions)

Liabilities and stockholders' equity

	2000	1999
Current liabilities:		
Short-term borrowings	711	453
Accounts payable	4,233	4,380
Deferred revenues	1,089	872
Other liabilities	5,516	6,033
Total current liabilities	11,549	11,838
Long-term debt	575	
Post retirement and other post employment benefits	652	605
Stockholders' equity		
Common stock	8,039	7,627
Retained earnings	5,347	4,948
Other income	27	2,919
	-1333	-660
Total stockholders' equity	12,080	14,834
Total liabilities and stockholder equity	24,856	27,277

Exhibit 12

Compaq Computer Corporation

Property, Plant and Equipment

(in millions)

December 31(in million)	2000	1999
Land	342	342
Buildings and leasehold improvements	1,493	1,572
Machinery and equipment	3,786	3,095
Equipment leased to third parties	1,166	741
Construction-in-process	261	301
	7,048	6,051
Less: Accumulated depreciation	(3,617)	(2,802)

John D. Sullivan, Ph.D.
Exhibit 13

Compaq Computer Corporation

Inventory

(in millions)

	2000	1999
Raw material	540	448
Work-in-progress	298	394
Finished goods	1,323	1,166
	2,161	2,008

Suggested Questions for Students

1. Why merge these two companies?

2. Given the US economy, is this the right time to be merging? Should they wait for the first sign of a turnaround?

3. Why has the HP stockholders reacted negatively, but not the shareholders from Compaq? Do you see any issues here?

4. If interest rates are so low, why go ahead with a stock swap? How does this transaction work and what advantages does it have?

5. Are these two companies a good fit? What overlap do they have? Do they have different reputations in the market? Will customers react one way or another?

6. Why is management continuing to push for the acquisition in light of the some of the institutional shareholders non-support of the deal?

7. With the stock price of Compaq falling, how does this impact the transaction? How has HP's stock price performed? Are they different? If so, why?

8. What synergies does Compaq bring to the table? Should these be used to value the new company? What's the danger here?

9. Should the shareholders of HP accept management's proposal? If you were on the Board, how would you vote?

MedImmune

MedImmune, Incorporated, a biotechnology company with five products on the market and a series of products in the pipeline, has considered expanding its operations and market power through the purchase of a smaller biotech firm that would compliment their existing product base.

In their search for a suitable candidate, the management of MedImmune began to target Aviron, a biopharmaceutical company based in Mountain View, California. While the company's lead product, FluMist, helped Aviron generate $11.7 million in revenue for the first nine months of 2001, it reported a net loss of $89.2 million for the same period. The company's goal is to become a leader in the discovery, development, manufacture, and marketing of vaccines that are safe, effective, and can be marketed to a large population.

While the acquisition looked like a fairly good strategic fit for MedImmune, the financial condition of the new biotechnology firm made a decision on an offer difficult to calculate.

Drug Cycles

For pharmaceutical and biotechnology companies to remain competitive, a continuous flow of new and improved drugs must be developed. Many companies start with a series of early possible drugs that have merit, but as research and clinical trials progress, many hopeful therapies are deemed ineffective and are either discarded, or part of the research is used in other areas for possible other products.

Drugs are considered to enter "phases" of development as they progress from hypothesis to manufacturing. At the earliest stage of testing, products are in Phase 1 and Phase 2 clinical trials. These clinical trials generally involve the administration of the drug to a small number of patients to examine the safety, dosage, and to a lesser extent, efficacy. Once the product has passed through Phase 1 and Phase 2 clinical trials, the drug enters Phase 3 where efficacy is tested. On average, it takes between ten to twelve years to bring a drug to market and the cost, depending on each product's complexity, can reach as high as $500 million.

MedImmune Background

Headquartered in Gaithersburg, Maryland, MedImmune presently has five products on the market and a wide portfolio of potential products in the research phase of development. The company uses its strength in advanced immunology and other areas of biology to target unmet needs in infectious diseases and patients suffering from immune deficiencies. The company also focuses on cancer treatment through its wholly owned subsidiary, MedImmune Oncology, inc. This subsidiary, formerly under the name Bioscience, Inc., was acquired in November 1999.[31]

Synagis

Approved by the Food and Drug Administration in 1998 for marketing, Synagis is prescribed for pediatric patients for the prevention of serious lower respiratory tract disease caused by respiratory syncytial virus. Administered by an injection, the drug is given once per month during anticipated times of disease prevalence.

CytoGam

To prevent cytomegalovirus in kidney, lung, liver, pancreas, and heart transplants, the company developed the intravenous drug CytoGam. Cytomegalovirus is a species specific herpes virus and usually is harmless. For those with immune deficiency system however, it may cause a fatal pneumonia.

With approximately 20,000 transplants in the United States each year, CytoGam has been shown through clinical studies to reduce cytomegalovirus by 56% in liver and 50% in kidney transplant patients.

---

[31] MedImmune, Inc. Securities and Exchange Form 10-K. December 30, 2000.

In 1993, the company began selling and marketing the drug through its hospital sales force. By 2000, sales of CytoGam reached $36.5 million in the United States.[32] Sales of the drug may increase as the supply of organs for transplant increases.

RespiGam

Approved by the Food and Drug Administration in 1996, RespiGam is an intravenous drug used to treat respiratory syncytial virus for small children. The company believes that the drug is largely being replaced by Synagis.

Ethyol

To prevent renal toxicity associated with patients being repeatedly administered with cisplatin for the treatment of ovarian cancer or non-small cell cancer, Ethyol acts as a cytoprotective agent. Ethyol was initially approved by the Food and Drug Administration in 1995 for the treatment of patients with ovarian cancer.

NeuTrexin

Approved in the United States and Canada in 1993, NeuTrexin is most commonly used as an anti-cancer agent as a treatment for Pneumocystis carinii pneumonia, a condition also experienced by patients that suffer from AIDS. However, due to the rapid improvement in the treatment of AIDS through new and improved drugs, the company has seen a slow decline in the use of NeuTrexin for AIDS patients.

In 1994, the European Union approved the use of NeuTrexin for patients suffering from Pneumocystis carinii pneumonia with compromised immune systems.

---

[32] MedImmune, Inc. Securities and Exchange Form 10-K. December 30, 2000.

John D. Sullivan, Ph.D.

Products Under Development

The company has a long line of products under development. A list of these products is listed in Exhibit 1.

Manufacturing

MedImmune's manufacturing facility is located in Frederick, Maryland and contains a large cell culture production area for the manufacture of products such as Synagis and MEDI-507, if it clears clinical trials and FDA approval. The company also maintains a small manufacturing facility in Nijmegan, the Netherlands.

Marketing

To market and sell the company's line of products, MedImmune employs 240 people dedicated to the United States with approximately 50 representatives covering 500 hospitals specializing in transplantation, pediatric, or neonatal care. These sales reps concentrate on the promotion of CytoGam, RespiGam, and Synagis. About 90 sales and marketing representatives cover the top 10,000 hospitals in the United States promoting Synagis and RespiGam. Other representatives that specialize in oncology and immunology market products such as Ethyol to physicians practicing in cancer treatment centers, large hospitals, and private practices.

MedImmune also utilizes Abbott labs' Ross Products division to co-promote its products in the United States. Ross Products employs roughly 500 sales representatives and promotes Synagis to 27,000 office-based pediatricians and 6,000 birth hospitals.

Sales made outside the United States are done through distributors. Abbot serves as the company's exclusive distribution company for Synagis. For Europe, Scherico sells and markets Ethyol. Other products such as CytoGam, Hexalen, NeuTrexin, and RespitGam were marketed and sold by various smaller distribution companies.

Employee Base

At year-end 2000, the company maintained a good relationship with its 790 full time employees.

Government Regulation

The research, development, and marketing of pharmaceuticals are subject to regulations set forth by the United States and other countries. In the United States, all drugs must be approved by the Food and Drug Administration and fall under several statutes and regulations including the Food, Drug and Cosmetics Act and the Public Health Service Act. The Food and Drug Administration also has the right to revoke product licenses.

To encourage research into areas of rare disease, the United States government enacted the Orphan Drug Act. Because the financial costs are typically so high to develop new drugs, many of these companies were searching for cures to mass disease rather than disease populations with less than 200,000 persons. Under this act, any company that receives Food and Drug Administration approval can potentially provide the company with market exclusivity for seven years. In addition, the company will receive tax credits up to 50% for qualified clinical research in these areas and the opportunity for clinical research grants.

Aviron Background

Aviron is a biopharmaceutical company that concentrates its efforts on the prevention of disease through innovative and cutting edge vaccine technology. The company's lead product for development and commercialization is FluMist, a live virus vaccine delivered to the patient as a nasal mist for the prevention of influenza. Research focuses on vaccine development programs that are based on producing weakened live vaccines and on its genetic engineering technologies. Weakened live virus vaccines have had a strong history in preventing disease such as smallpox, polio, measles, mumps, rubella, and chicken pox.

FluMist

FluMist, Aviron's primary product, has undergone and continues to undergo clinical trials. Many of these trials are coordinated with the National Institute of Health investigators. FluMist has been tested in 24,000 healthy children and adults and has been generally shown to provide a protection against influenza. Typical side effects of the treatment were sore throat, nasal decongestion, and a slight fever.

The Biologics License Application, or BLA, for frozen FluMist was submitted to the United States Food and Drug Administration in October 2000. In September 2001, the FDA requested additional information regarding clinical and manufacturing data from the company.

Other Aviron Research
PIV-3

PIV-3 is a common childhood respiratory virus that causes croup, cough, fever and pneumonia. For children in the United States, more than 60% are infected by the age of two and 80% of those who contract the disease do so by age four. Aviron is presently engaged in the research and development of a vaccine to treat this disease.

CMV

A member of the herpes virus family, CMV infections can result in mild symptoms such as a sore throat, headache, fatigue and swollen glands. In more drastic cases of infection, CMV can diminish the strength of the immune system and can often be found in patients with AIDS, cancer, and transplant patients.

Conclusion

The board of MedImmune believed that Aviron was a good strategic fit but didn't know what to offer. While the company had some attractive features, it still lacked positive earnings and cash flow to generate traditional financial value. They didn't want to insult the management of Aviron with a low offer, but also felt the pressure to offer an appropriate price. It had also been their experience that a purchase like this one was better done as a friendly transaction.

John D. Sullivan, Ph.D.
Exhibit 1

MedImmune

Products Under Development

Product	Indication
Synais RSV Marketed	Prevention of RSV disease
CytoGam Marketed	Prophylaxis of cytomegalovirus
RespiGam Marketed	Prevention of serious RSV
Ethyol Marketed	Reduction of cumulative renal toxicity
Ethyol Marketed	Reduction of the incidence of severe xerostomia
NeuTrexin Marketed	Alternative treatment of Pneumocystis carinii pneumonia
Synagis RSV Phase 3	RSV disease in bone marrow transplant
Synagis RSV Phase 4	Prevention of RSV children under 2 years
Synagis RSV Phase 3	Children under 2 years with congenital heart disease
Ethyol Phase 3	Treatment of NSCLC
Ethyol Phase 2/3	Reduction in radiotherapy
Neutrexin Phase 3	Treatment of colorectal cancer
MEDI-507 Phase 1	Treatment of graft-versus-host disease
MEDI-507 Phase 2	Treatment of psoriasis
Ethyol Phase 2/3	Head and neck cancer
MEDI-491 Phase 1	Prevention of B19 parvovirus infection
UTI Vaccine Phase 2	Prevention of urinary tract
HPV Cervical Cancer	Prevention of cervical cancer
Vitaxin Anti Phase 1	Treatment of cancer
Numax Preclinical	Prevention of RSV disease

Exhibit 2

MedImmune

Stock Performance

	2000		1999	
	High	**Low**	**High**	**Low**
First Quarter	76.25	43	22	14.33
Second Quarter	80.69	42	24.67	15
Third Quarter	86.13	57.75	40.21	22.96
Fourth Quarter	72.63	44.63	58.6	29.67
Year End Close	47.69		55.29	

John D. Sullivan, Ph.D.
Exhibit 3

MedImmune

Product Sales

Product Sales (In Million)	2000	1999
Synagis	427	293
CytoGam	36.5	34.7
Ethyol	21.4	19.6
Other Products	10.9	9.5
Total	495.8	356.8

Exhibit 4

MedImmune

Total Assets

	31-Dec-00	31-Dec-99
Assets		
Cash	84,974	36,570
Marketable securities	406,455	214,750
Trade receivable, net	115,635	86,894
Inventory, net	46,633	31,777
Deferred tax assets	22,319	23,132
Other current assets	11,796	8,715
Total Current Assets	687,812	401,838
Property and equipment, net	86,383	87,452
Deferred tax assets, net	194,761	128,990
Marketable securities	34,825	19,074
Other assets	2,794	11,070
Total Assets	1,006,575	648,424

John D. Sullivan, Ph.D.
Exhibit 5

MedImmune

Liabilities

	2000	1999
Accounts payable, trade	3,090	2,995
Accrued expenses	72,159	65,300
Product royalties payable	40,553	28,527
Deferred revenue	33,966	
Other current liabilities	1,697	2,130
Total Current Liabilities	151,465	98,952
Long-term debt	9,595	10,366
Other liabilities	1,933	2,027
Total Liabilities	162,993	111,345

Exhibit 6

MedImmune

Statement of Operations

Revenues

	2000	1999
Product sales	495,803	356,815
Other revenue	44,692	26,560
Total revenues	540,495	383,375

Costs and Expenses

	2000	1999
Cost of sales	127,320	90,193
Research and development	66,296	59,565
Selling, administrative and general	157,330	139,389
Other operating expenses	9,231	17,409
Total expenses	360,177	306,556
Operating income (loss)	180,318	76,819

John D. Sullivan, Ph.D.
Exhibit 7

Aviron

Stock Performance

Year Ended December 31, 1999

First Quarter	26.75	17.50
Second Quarter	28.75	17.13
Third Quarter	34.06	21.00
Fourth Quarter	28.75	14.81

Year Ended December 31, 2000

First Quarter	54.38	15.00
Second Quarter	35.00	21.00
Third Quarter	59.00	27.56
Fourth Quarter	70.61	46.00

Exhibit 8

Aviron

Assets

	1999	2000
Current Assets:		
Cash and cash equivalents	28,081	64,662
Short-term investments	24,235	67,651
Accounts receivable	3,241	23,288
Inventory	2,082	4,264
Other current assets	1,009	2,691
Total current assets	58,648	162,556
Long-term investments		4,506
Property and equipment, net	25,635	27,707
Intangible assets, net		48,046
Deposits and other assets	7,411	5,924
Total Assets	91,694	248,739

John D. Sullivan, Ph.D.
Exhibit 9

Aviron

Liabilities

Liabilities and stockholders' equity(deficit)

	1999	2000
Current Liabilities:		
Accounts payable	3,038	5,106
Accrued compensation	1,739	4,978
Accrued clinical trial costs	846	1,974
Accrued interest	1,438	695
Accrued expenses and other liabilities	6,591	7,654
Current portion of capital lease obligations	101	9
Current portion of long term obligations	2,680	5,945
Total current liabilities	16,433	26,361
Deferred rent	2,214	2,095
Deferred revenue		9,750
Capital lease obligations, less current portion	9	
Long-term obligations, less current portion	112,657	89,947

Exhibit 10

Aviron

Stockholder Equity

	1999	2000
Preferred stock		
Common stock	17	25
Paid-in capital	143,822	394,012
Notes receivable	-83	-50
Deferred compensation	-96	
Accumulated deficit	-183,279	-273,401
Total stockholders' equity (deficit)	-39,619	120,586
Total liabilities and stockholder's equity	91,694	248,739

John D. Sullivan, Ph.D.
Exhibit 11

Aviron

Statement of Operations

	Year Ended December 31		
	1998	1999	2000
Revenues:			
Contract revenue and grants	745	22,232	32,242
Operating Expenses:			
Research and development	46,583	68,121	80,521
Acquisition of in-process research and development			10,904
General, administrative and marketing	10,085	13,159	13,849
Total Operating Expenses	56,668	81,371	105,174
Loss from Operations	-55,923	-59,139	-73,032
Other Income(Expense)			
Interest income	6,003	3,633	6,541
Interest expense	-4,882	-6,364	-11,020
Total Other Income(expense), net	1,121	-2,731	-4,479
Net Loss	-54,802	-61,870	-77,511

Exhibit 12

Aviron

Investments

	Cost	Gross	Gross Unrealized Loses	Market Value
As of December 31, 1999				
Corporate commercial paper	4,386	25		4,411
U.S. corporate notes	9,251		-139	9,112
U.S. corporate bonds	9,385	3	-40	9,348
U.S. government agency obligations	1,004		-13	991
Municipal bonds	1,810		-9	1,801
	25,836	28	-201	25,663
As of December 31, 2000				
Corporate commercial paper	72,894	26	-65	72,855
U.S. corporate bonds	23,189	45	-52	23,182
U.S. government agency obligations	2,000	12		2,012
	98,083	83	-117	98,049

John D. Sullivan, Ph.D.
Exhibit 13

Aviron

Property and Equipment

	1999	2000
Property and Equipment		
Manufacturing equipment	5,978	6,551
Laboratory equipment	5,992	7,780
Computer equipment	3,113	4,219
Office equipment	1,070	1,202
Leasehold improvements	18,930	19,856
Construction in progress	280	3,704
	35,363	43,312
Less accumulated depreciation and amortization	-9,728	-15,605
Net Property and Equipment	25,635	27,707

Case Studies in Mergers & Acquisitions

Suggested Questions for Students

1. Are these companies a good fit?

2. Do you see good overlap in the type of research they're conducting?

3. Why would MedImmune be interested in purchasing Aviron if they already have products in the pipeline?

4. How would you value Aviron if they don't have any positive earnings or cash flow?

5. What's the risk in using a discounted cash flow model?

6. How would you compensate for risk?

7. If Aviron's drugs take off and you see rapid growth in sales in the next few years, how should you forecast this growth in the out years of the model based on what you've read in the case?

8. If you sat on MedImmune's board of directors, would you approve of the merger? What price should be offered based on your discounted cash flow? Is this an insult to Aviron

Willamette

In the fall of 2000, Weyerhaeuser Company, one of the worlds largest integrated timber companies, made an offer to purchase Willamette Industries, also a large integrated timber company, for $48 per share in cash. After three days of consideration, the board of Willamette rejected Weyerhaeuser's offer citing that the price, valued at $5.3 billion, did not accurately reflect the value of the company or its future growth potential. The immediate rejection, which many in the industry expected, placed Weyerhaeuser in the position of deciding whether or not to initiate a hostile takeover attempt.

After two weeks of consideration, Weyerhaeuser announced that it would launch a hostile takeover of the company settling on a price of $50 per share. For months, Willamette considered the offer with several rejections along the way and an announcement that it would purchase roughly ten million shares in a ongoing share repurchase program that would continue depending on stock price.

Finally, on January 2, 2002, Weyerhaeuser raised its bid to $55 per share and stated that it was as high as it could go. Two days later, Willamette Industries announced that the price was inadequate and that it was terminating its discussions regarding Weyerhaeuser's acquisition offers.

Was the deal over? Weyerhaeuser knew that the synergies and potential fit were superb. Was it just a question of raising the price or not? Weyerhaeuser, if they really wanted Willamette, needed to decide whether or not to go back to the negotiation table and force a takeover with a price that both could accept.

Background

Willamette Industries

Established in 1906 in Dallas, Oregon, Willamette Valley Lumber company grew into one of the largest integrated timber companies in the world with 105 manufacturing facilities in 24 states, France, Ireland, and Mexico.

John D. Sullivan, Ph.D.

Business Segments

Paper

Willamette produces a wide range of paper and paper products for internal and external customers. For white paper, the company's four paper mills manufacture 11% of the U.S. uncoated free sheet production and 8% of the country's bleached hardwood market pulp.

Through six cut sheet facilities, the company also manufactures 23% of the nation's communication paper and utilizes several brands including its private Willamette name brand.

The company also manufactures several brown paper products including linerboard, bag paper, and cardboard sheets for boxes. Willamette's four bag plants produce 14% of the country's paper bags.

Building Materials

The Building Material business segment is divided into four primary types of products: Lumber, Structural Panels, Composite Panels, and Engineered Wood Products.

Through the company's nine sawmills, the lumber products are marketed through independent wholesalers and distributors throughout the United States. As of December 31, 2000, the company held approximately 2% of the country's lumber production.

Plywood panels and oriented strand board are manufactured at one plant and account for approximately 8% and 3% of the US production of structural panels. Like lumber, these products are marketed through independent wholesalers and distributors throughout the United States.

Through four particleboard plants, the company manufactures approximately 14% of the US market. A smaller plant in France manufactures approximately 1% of European production. Three other plants produce medium density fiberboard and manufacture approximately 22% of the US market. These products are also sold and marketed through independent wholesalers and distributors.

Case Studies in Mergers & Acquisitions

The Engineered Wood Product segment has three primary products: Laminated beams, laminated veneer lumber, and I-joist products. Through two plants, the laminated beam production accounts for 24% of US production. Three laminated veneer plants produce nearly 11% of the market production and through two I-joist facilities, the company makes approximately 9% of the total US market production. These products are sold both in the domestic and international markets.

Timber Assets

Approximately 69% of Willamette's long-term saw log needs come from the company's 1,729,000 acres of timberland located in Louisiana, Texas, Arkansas, Oregon, Tennessee, Missouri, and the Carolinas. The balance of the company's timber needs come from private timber sales in the open market.

Energy Consumption

The manufacturing of timber products, by its very nature, tends to consume a tremendous amount of energy. To cope with these costs, Willamette facilities are able to generate 61% of their energy needs through the burning of waste materials and the recycling of pulping liquors.

Employees

At year-end 2000, Willamette employed approximately 14,975 persons with nearly 45% of these employees represented by labor unions and collective bargaining agreements. One agreement with approximately 1,640 employees expired in 200 and was renegotiated.

The company has experienced very little turnover in the salary level positions. Approximately 46% of these employees have been with the company for at least twelve years.

John D. Sullivan, Ph.D.

Weyerhaeuser

Incorporated in 1900, Weyerhaeuser is one of the world's largest integrated forest products companies with offices and or operations in 17 countries and an employee base of 47,244. The focus of the company has been to grow and harvest timber for the sale and distribution of forest products, and real estate development and construction.

The company is principally divided into four business segments: Timberlands, Wood Products, Pulp, Paper, & Packaging, and Real Estate and related assets.

Timberlands

Weyerhaeuser manages 5.9 million acres of company owned land and .5 million acres of leased land in North America. The timber in these acres produces mostly high quality lumber and related products for distribution in the United States and in the International markets. The company also has several renewable and long-term licenses for 31.6 million acres throughout Canada. The inventory of timber in these areas is approximately 588 million cunits.[33] To ensure a steady quality and quantity of timber, the company has an extensive planting of high quality trees and suppresses those species of tree that cannot be brought to market.

Wood Products

Weyerhaeuser produces and sells hardwood lumber, treated lumber, plywood and veneer, softwood lumber, engineered wood, and composite panels. These products are predominately by the company's internal sales force.

---

[33] Each cunit represents 100 cubic feet of solid timber.

Pulp, Paper, & Packaging

The company manufactures chemical wood pulp for distribution throughout the world, paper products that include both coated and uncoated papers, and containerboard sheets for packaging.

Real Estate and Related Assets

Through the company's subsidiary, Weyerhaeuser Real Estate Company, the company develops and constructs single-family houses for sale including large planned communities.

Conclusion

Weyerhaeuser management knew the dangers of betting too much on synergies for valuation. There was just no way of knowing if the potential cost savings and efficiencies could be realized in the time necessary to ensure the transaction would add to earnings upon competition. However, it was also believed that the purchase would also make Weyerhaeuser a global timber giant and management desperately wanted to do the deal. The only question was whether or not $55 per share was really the most they could afford and if they could raise the offer based on updates to a discounted cash flow model using several discount rates from 12% to 15%.

John D. Sullivan, Ph.D.

Exhibit 1

Willamette

Income Statement

(in thousands)

	2000	1999	1998
Net Sales	$4,651,761	$4,272,957	$3,880,249
Expenses			
Depr\Amort & Cost of Fee Timber	$314,999	$303,719	$371,141
Materials, Labor, & Other Operating	$3,414,686	$3,165,275	$3,006,572
Gross Profit	$922,076	$803,963	$502,536
Selling and Administration	$268,819	$253,694	$239,792
Other Income\Expense	($19,737)	($11,710)	$2,029
Operating Earnings	$633,520	$538,559	$264,773
Interest Expense	$119,133	$125,284	$131,990
Earnings before Tax	$514,387	$413,275	$132,783
Income Tax	$169,500	$152,800	$43,800
Net Earnings	$344,887	$260,475	$88,983

Exhibit 2

Willamette

Financial Snapshot

(in thousands)

	2000	**1999**	**1998**
Capital Expenditures	$398,888	$290,246	$441,839
Working Capital	$396,094	$457,471	$366,846
Long Term Debt	$1,542,926	$1,628,843	$1,821,083
Total Debt	$1,670,425	$1,645,716	$1,870,602
Total Assets	$5,117,670	$4,797,861	$4,697,668
Shares Outstanding	109,417	111,587	110,981

John D. Sullivan, Ph.D.

Exhibit 3

Willamette

Assets

(in thousands)

2000

Current Assets

Cash	$24,284
A\R	$459,591
Inventory	$473,788
Prepaid Expenses	$35,154

Total Current Assets $992,817

Timber & Related Facilities	$1,014,285
Property, Plant, & Equip	$3,017,593
Other Assets	$92,975

Total Assets $5,117,670

Exhibit 4

Willamette

Liabilities and Shareholder Equity

(in thousands)

2000

Current Liabilities

Current Portion of LT Debt	$5,499
Notes Payable	$122,000
A\P	$253,292
Accrued Payroll	$85,084
Accrued Interest	$33,910
Other Accrued Expenses	$77,754
Accrued Income Tax	$19,184
Total Current Liabilities	**$596,723**
Deferred Income Tax	$568,273
Other Liabilities	$28,705
Long Term Debt	$1,542,926
Stockholder's Equity	$54,709
Capital Surplus	$229,598
Retained Earnings	$2,096,736
Total Stockholders Equity	**$2,381,043**
Liabilities & Stockholder Equity	**$5,117,670**

John D. Sullivan, Ph.D.
Exhibit 5

Willamette

Quarterly Snapshot

(in thousands)

2000	Net Sales	Gross Profit
1st Quarter	$1,167,126	$224,163
2nd Quarter	$1,188,060	$240,358
3rd Quarter	$1,169,585	$226,052
4th Quarter	$1,126,990	$231,503
	$4,657,761	$922,076

1999	Net Sales	Gross Profit
1st Quarter	$970,483	$141,942
2nd Quarter	$1,056,319	$195,757
3rd Quarter	$1,137,615	$239,780
4th Quarter	$1,108,540	$226,484
	$4,272,957	$803,963

1998	Net Sales	Gross Profit
1st Quarter	$942,384	$120,761
2nd Quarter	$991,509	$125,578
3rd Quarter	$1,003,242	$148,476
4th Quarter	$943,114	$107,721
	$3,880,249	$502,536

Exhibit 6

Willamette

Property, Plant, & Equipment

(in thousands)

	2000	**1999**
Land	$48,436	$41,985
Buildings	$417,700	$380,967
Machinery & Equipment	$4,924,423	$4,569,273
Furniture & Fixtures	$96,597	$92,411
Leasehold Improvements	$8,023	$6,619
Construction in Progress	$236,950	$145,479
Total	$5,732,129	$5,236,734
Less Accumulated Depreciation	$2,714,536	$2,485,524
Net Property, Plant, & Equipment	$3,017,593	$2,751,210

John D. Sullivan, Ph.D.

Suggested Questions for Students

1. Are the synergies proposed for Willamette realistic?

2. What is an accurate valuation for Willamette?

3. At $55 per share, is the deal dilutive or accretive for Weyerhaeuser?

Everest Healthcare Services Corporation

Everest Healthcare Services Corporation, the sixth largest provider of dialysis in the United States, had been contemplating a merger with the largest provider of dialysis service and products in the world, Fresenius Medical Care. The only question was whether or not this was the right time and what should be the correct price?

Background

The United States health care system, under a continuing pressure brought on by cost constraints, had been in a constant strategy of consolidation to leverage purchasing power and reduce administrative expenditures. As an additional benefit, larger service providers with a significant patient population had leverage in negotiating with third party commercial payers. For smaller health care organizations, it was usually only a matter of time before it was necessary for acquisition talks to begin. Simply, the infrastructure above providing direct patient care became too costly.

End Stage Renal Disease

Currently, there are only three types of treatment for ESRD: hemodialysis, peritoneal dialysis, and kidney transplantation. Transplants are limited by the scarcity of compatible kidneys. Approximately 12,200 patients received kidney transplants in the United States during 1996.[34] Therefore, most patients must rely on dialysis, which is the process of removing toxins and excess water by artificial means. The primary types of treatment options for dialysis patients are hemodialysis and peritoneal dialysis and are based on the patient's medical conditions and needs.

---

[34] United States Renal Data System: USRDS 1999 Renal Data Report. National Institutes of Health, National Institutes of Diabetes and Digestive and Kidney Disease. Bethesda, MD 1999 pp. 102-112

John D. Sullivan, Ph.D.

Hemodialysis is utilized by roughly 83% of all kidney failure patients and involves three treatments per week in an outpatient clinic, hospital clinic, or in the home.[35] Each treatment, depending on the individual patient's prescription and condition, will last for approximately three or four hours. During this treatment, the blood flows outside the body by means of plastic tubes known as bloodlines into a specially designed membrane filter, a dialyzer, which functions as an artificial kidney by separating waste products and excess water from the blood by diffusion and ultra filtration. Dialysis solution caries away the waste products and excess water, and clean blood is returned to the patient. The movement of blood and dialysis solution is controlled by a hemodialysis machine, which pumps blood, adds anti-coagulants, regulates the purification process and controls the mixing of dialysis solution and the rate of its flow through the system. These machines also monitor the patient's progress and vital signs. Of the roughly 156 treatments per year, 144 usually take place in the outpatient setting. The remainder is usually performed during hospital stays. Roughly 70% of hemodialysis patients are treated in independent (non-hospital) outpatient facilities that specialize in dialysis. Large chains own about half of these private clinics.[36] The remaining patients are serviced in hospital outpatient dialysis centers that are generally older, outdated, and less appealing because they are in the midst of acutely ill patients. The majority of hemodialysis patients are referred to outpatient clinics, where hemodialysis treatments are performed with the assistance of a nurse or dialysis technician under the general supervision of a physician. Hemodialysis is the only form of treatment other than transplantation currently available to patients who have low residual or nonexistent renal function and are inadequately dialyzed using peritoneal dialysis.

Peritoneal dialysis accounts for the remaining approximately 15% of the patient base. Peritoneal dialysis or PD, removes waste products from the blood by use of the peritoneum, the membrane lining

---

[35] United States Renal Data System: USRDS 1999 Renal Data Report. National Institutes of Health, National Institutes of Diabetes and Digestive and Kidney Disease. Bethesda, MD 1999
[36] United States Renal Data System: USRDS 1999 Renal Data Report. National Institutes of Health, National Institutes of Diabetes and Digestive and Kidney Disease. Bethesda, MD 1999

covering the internal organs located in the abdominal area. Most peritoneal dialysis patients are self administered by patients in their own homes and workplaces. There are presently two types of peritoneal treatments: continuous ambulatory peritoneal dialysis (CAPD) and continuous cycling peritoneal dialysis (CCPD). In both of these treatments, the patient has a catheter surgically implanted to provide access to the peritoneal cavity. Using this catheter, a sterile dialysis solution is introduced into the peritoneal cavity and the peritoneum operates as the dialyzing membrane. CAPD is used by 75% of PD patients and involves the administration and draining of a total of eight liters of dialysis solutions in and out of the peritoneum several times each day.[37] Osmosis causes toxins and excess body fluids to flow into the solutions and dissolve there. The fluid is usually drained hours later and the process is repeated several times in each 24-hour period. In general, patients go about their activities carrying the excess fluid inside and are constantly monitoring or administering the procedure. Because the PD procedure is performed daily, it consumes far more solutions and drainage tubing than is required for hemodialysis.

CCPD is used by 25% of PD patients and is performed while the patient sleeps. A cycler machine, connected to the peritoneum by a catheter attached tubing set, adds and drains roughly 15 liters of dialysis solution to and from the abdomen.[38]

Both CAPD and CCPD are performed daily and the patient typically does not experience the buildup of toxins and fluids experienced by hemodialysis patients on the days they are not treated. In addition, because the patient isn't required to make frequent visits to a dialysis clinic and the patient can make solution exchanges at more convenient times, the disruption on a patient's personal life is far less than that of a hemodialysis patient. Certain aspects of peritoneal dialysis, however, limit its use as a long-term treatment therapy for some patients. First, certain patients have difficulty sterilizing connections of the peritoneal dialysis tubing to the catheter, leading to excessive episodes of peritonitis, a bacterial infection of the peritoneum, which can result in serious adverse health consequences, including death. Second,

---

[37] HCFA Bureau of Data Management and Strategy. Health Care Financing Research Report: End Stage Renal Disease, 1994. Department of Health and Human Services, September 1996
[38] Ibid.

treatment by current forms of peritoneal dialysis may not be as effective in removing wastes and fluids as hemodialysis.[39] As a result, patients using peritoneal dialysis must have some residual renal function or the therapy must be increased. In general, residual renal function decreases leading patients to eventually change treatment therapies from peritoneal to hemodialysis.

Pursuant to Health Care Financing Administration (HCFA) and Medicare regulations, outpatient dialysis clinics serve as supervisory agents for peritoneal patients. In effect, clinicians administer the dialysis "prescription" by initially training the patient to perform the treatment in the clinic and later providing supplies and solutions and monitoring the patient through a regular battery of testing.

Both of these forms of peritoneal dialysis place considerable responsibility for care on the patient, who is required to keep precise treatment records and pay particular attention to sterile technique to avoid infection (the incidence of which remains very high). Over the past 12 years, the number of dialysis patients using PD has grown about 12% per year.[40] Given the increased frequency of treatments, PD procedures utilize substantially more disposable supplies than do hemodialysis treatments. Being far less labor intensive however, PD, which is billed at the same reimbursement rate, can significantly lower costs for the provider.

End Stage Renal Disease: A Non Working Model for National Health Care in the United States

The real debate over the possibility of a national end stage renal disease program began in 1970 before becoming part of the United States Medicare Program in 1973. Unlike the present day, the stakeholders involved in kidney disease in the late 60's and early 70's were primarily held to only patients, families, and physicians. Today that list has expanded to include large dialysis chains, smaller less efficient

---

[39] United States Renal Data System: USRDS 1999 Renal Data Report. National Institutes of Health, National Institutes of Diabetes and Digestive and Kidney Disease. Bethesda, MD 1999 pp. 40-41

[40] HCFA Bureau of Data Management and Strategy. Health Care Financing Research Report: End Stage Renal Disease, 1994. Department of Health and Human Services, September 1996

Case Studies in Mergers & Acquisitions

service companies, integrated supply companies, health maintenance organizations, stockholders, and with a greater presence than ever before, the pharmaceutical industry.

But it is not uncommon for policies implemented by a governing body to change over time. Similar to any living entity, a policy will evolve based on different experiences and circumstances that impact those directly involved in the success, failure or continuation of that policy.

During the 1970 hearings before the Sub Committee on Public Health and Welfare of the House of Representatives, several expert opinions from the medical field painted a picture of how a "nationalized" kidney disease program should take shape and why this particular program would succeed. Most, including politicians, placed the concern of the patients before all other considerations. Further, many argued, with the help of technology and innovation, costs for providing this care would significantly come down making the government's investment smaller over time benefiting both the patient, as well as the tax payers.

But the policy was to do more than merely treat the end result of a series of different ailments such as diabetes. If the model worked correctly and was properly funded and supported, diseases leading to ESRD could be treated thus eliminating the need for dialysis or transplantation.

In 1974, not even a full year after the program was implemented, the House of Representatives held hearings to determine the feasibility of a policy to provide national health insurance for the U.S. population. While the initial perspective of the ESRD program was considered a financial success only spending $229 million[41] in its first twelve months, significant implementation problems haunted the program throughout the first year. The most critical problem related to an underestimate of the potential patient population and supply of available nephrologists.

Does the ESRD program serve as a model for other segments in health care? End Stage Renal Disease, while it covers a specific segment of the population that desperately needs care, lacks the applicability to other segments in health care. End Stage Renal Disease, by its very definition, is the end

---

[41] United States General Accounting Office. Health, Education, and Human Services Division. <u>Medicare: Enrollment Growth and Payment Practices for Kidney Dialysis Services.</u> November 1995. p. 1

result of other ailments such as hypertension and diabetes. Presently there is no cure for kidney disease and while the optimal treatment continues to be transplantation, this therapy is still only considered to be a treatment rather than a cure.

An additional problem with the policy has been cost. While Medicare has repeatedly reduced the reimbursement rate for the treatment, overall costs have skyrocketed as the patient population has continued to grow net of mortality as the rates of diabetes and hypertension have continued to expand throughout the general United States population. Medicare expenditures on dialysis have grown since 1993 from $7.12 billion to $10.77 billion in 1997.[42]

Has the End Stage Renal Disease Program been a success? Some health care policy analysts hail the program as the "model" for U.S. health care while others believe the present program is severely broken and in dire need of repair. But with mortality rates hovering above 20%, it is difficult to argue that the program has been an absolute success. However, without the program, thousands of patients certainly would have perished without this life saving therapy. So with regards to treating "patients with dialysis," the program has accomplished this one of many goals set in place thirty years ago.

But if the program is to live up to its full intentions, changes in how the program operates must be implemented. Transplantation, a mainstay of the original policy, has floundered due to a severe lack of organs and an illogical reimbursement policy that encourages organ rejection. The government can easily solve this problem by simply promoting organ donation and paying for immunosuppressive drugs for the life of the patient assuming the person has converted over to Medicare dialysis coverage. Aside from the obvious benefits to the patient and their family, from a financial perspective this course of action also makes sense.

Innovation and technology, with the exception of some pharmaceuticals, has been driven to reduce costs and from the perspective of the initial policy intent, has been a success. However, the focus should not entirely be dedicated to cost saving measures. If Medicare truly wishes to reduce dialysis expenditures,

---

[42] United States Renal Data System: USRDS 1999 Renal Data Report. National Institutes of Health, National Institutes of Diabetes and Digestive and Kidney Disease. Bethesda, MD 1999 pp. 151

the direction of technology and innovation needs to point at reducing the numbers of patients added to the program each year. An effective treatment of diabetes and hypertension may significantly reduce the number of new patients that require dialysis and thus, further reduce expenditures and also benefit patients.

From a reimbursement perspective, it may be unwise for a multi-billion dollar industry to operate at a loss on its base revenue, but reap its only profits from the sale of a single drug. If, under the direction of the Health Care Financing Administration, Medicare lowers the reimbursement rate by $1.00 per 1,000 units of the drug EPO, it is uncertain whether or not such a change in reimbursement policy would have a "material" impact on dialysis providers. Driven by profits, it is fairly obvious that the large dialysis chains would argue that any adverse change in EPO reimbursement policy would have a significant impact on earnings. If the Health Care Financing Administration intends to encourage an adjustment of the current rate of $10.00 per 1,000, the agency may also want to consider the impact this may have on the entire financial structure of the providers. In other words, if the impact on the industry is severe, a compromise between raising the composite rate in addition to lowering the EPO reimbursement rate may seem more reasonable.

The End Stage Renal Disease Industry

The treatment of kidney failure in the United States can be characterized into two general categories: Health Care Providers and Medical Product Manufacturers. To maintain and improve market share however, these two, at one time distinct, industry segments have also began to consolidate.

According to HCFA, in 1996 there were approximately 3,082 Medicare certified ESRD treatment centers in the United States. Ownership of these centers was fragmented. As of 1996, the ten largest providers of dialysis accounted for approximately 1,500 facilities (49% of the facilities) and care for 108,000 patients (50% of the patient population). Privately owned freestanding clinics represented 27% of the facilities and hospital based clinics accounted for the remaining 23%.[43]

[43] Ibid, pp. 165-171

John D. Sullivan, Ph.D.

The dialysis industry has experienced significant consolidation in recent years. Large chains have continued to purchase small to medium independent operators and chains. In 1994, National Medical Care, the largest provider of dialysis in the United States, acquired several dialysis centers for a total of $145.3 million in cash.[44] Over the next 12 months, National Medical Care increased their acquisitions, spending $260.8 million by the end of 1995. By contrast, the second largest provider of dialysis services, Vivra, spent only $4.3 million in dialysis related acquisitions in 1994.[45]

Small public companies have entered the dialysis market and have offered stock to acquisition targets, which has further accelerated the consolidation process. For example, in 1994, Renal Treatment Centers (Purchased by Total Renal Care in 1998) spent $50.3 million in cash, issued 87,608 shares of common stock valued at approximately $1.8 million and issued a $7.5 million dollar note for seven acquisitions completed during the year. These acquired centers provided care to approximately 1,373 patients.[46]

Because of this increased consolidation, the availability of acquisition targets has decreased significantly. Part of the consolidation attractiveness to chains has been the ability to group additional facilities under a centralized management system. This centralized system allows the provider to hold a tighter control over the expenses and operation of individual facilities. For example, billing may be conducted for several states through one location providing the dialysis chain with increased personnel cost savings. However, this does not mean that the corporate office dictates prescriptions for dialysis patients. Each facility conducts its operations, in large part, upon the applicable laws, rules and regulations of the jurisdiction in which the center is located. A patient's physician, either affiliated with the provider or a physician with staff privileges, has medical discretion as to the particular treatment modality and medications to be prescribed for the patient. Similarly, the attending physician has the authority in selecting particular medical products for each patient.

---

[44] W.R. Grace, 1994 Annual Report, p. 37
[45] Vivra, 1994 Annual Report, p. 17
[46] Renal Treatment Centers, 1994 Annual Report, p. 14

Case Studies in Mergers & Acquisitions

Acquisitions of these centers, primarily by larger chains or operators of smaller physician owed clinics, range widely with regards to purchase price. "Purchasing terms are usually based on potential revenue, i.e., number of regular patients in the facilities. Prices range from $10,000 to $40,000 per patient. During 1988-89, one hospital in Ohio bought a unit with 50 patients for $2.3 million, i.e., $46,000 per patients. The average purchase price in 1988, however, was estimated at $18,000 to $20,000 per patient. Prices apparently fell in 1989 to an estimated range of $15,000 to $18,000 per patient; changes in federal income tax law, quite independent of ESRD, significantly slowed corporate acquisitions. In states without CON (Certificate of Need) regulations, the prices tend to be lower."[47]

Everest Healthcare Services

Everest Healthcare Services began operations in 1968 with one dialysis facility and grew by acquisition and de novo facilities to become the sixth largest ESRD provider in the United States serving over 6,400 patients in 68 clinics in 12 states. As an additional revenue stream, the company also provides acute dialysis services to 30 hospitals in four states. Through contracts with 81 hospitals in 9 states, Everest also provides a wide range of extracorporeal blood treatment services such as perfusion, apheresis, and auto-transfusion. The company also provides management assistance to dialysis facilities that Everest either has a minority ownership interest in or is unaffiliated. This business segment is mostly located in the Chicago and northwest Indiana. As of September 1999, the company derived 86.9% of revenue from chronic and acute dialysis services, 11.7% from extracorporeal blood treatment services, and 1.4% from management contract services. A summary of the company's financial performance is located in exhibits 1 through 4.

Everest's dialysis operations have grown over the past three decades through 19 acquisitions adding 34 facilities to the company network of facilities. In addition, the company built 34 de novo facilities

---

[47] Rettig, R.A., and Levinsky, N.G. Kidney Failure and the Federal Government, Committee for the Study of the Medicare End Stage Renal Disease Program, National Academy Press, 1991, pp. 130

bringing the total Everest dialysis clinics to 68. Through its geographical tight network of facilities, the company has been able to leverage its relationships with physician groups and local hospitals. In addition to providing in center dialysis treatment, 56 of Everest's clinics also provide home dialysis training. 12 clinics provide exclusive home dialysis training and support.[48]

As of September 1999, the company operated 939 dialysis stations, for an average of 16 hours a day, and six days a week. Based on the in center patient base as of September 1999, the company maintained a dialysis station utilization rate of approximately 80%.[49]

Fresenius Medical Care

Fresenius Medical Care is the largest service and product provider for dialysis in the United States and the world. In 1999, the company treated 62,000 patients in 849 clinics in the US and 18,000 patients in 241 clinics in Europe, Asia, and Latin America. Total treatments in the United States grew from 7.2 million in 1997 to 8.9 million in 1999. International treatments were 1.9 million in 1997 growing to 2.5 million by 1999. The North American segment of Fresenius Medical Care accounted for 73% of total revenues.[50]

As with most dialysis businesses in the United States and abroad, Fresenius, in addition to realizing growth through its base business, grew through acquisitions. In 1999, the company acquired 36 dialysis clinics with 21 of the total acquired clinics located in Western Europe and Latin America. Spending for these clinics was $101 million compared with acquisition spending of $223 million in 1998. The company's acquisition strategy is to allocate approximately half of free cash flow to consolidation spending.

In January of 2000, Fresenius settled with the U.S. Government over an investigation involving National Medical Care, a former subsidiary of W.R. Grace later sold to Fresenius AG. The investigation, under the Office of Inspector General of the U.S. Department of Health and Human Services, involved, among other things, the billing practices of National Medical Care's dialysis and lab businesses. Under the

---

[48] Everest Healthcare Services. Securities and Exchange Form 10K. 1999
[49] Everest Healthcare Services. Securities and Exchange Form 10K. 1999
[50] Fresenius Medical Care. 1999 Annual Report.

Case Studies in Mergers & Acquisitions

settlement, Fresenius was required to pay the United States Government $486 million. At the time of the settlement, this was the largest health care settlement in U.S. history.

In 1997, Fresenius Medical Care partnered with the Renal Research Institute through the Beth Israel Medical Center in New York. Utilizing over 17 dialysis units in five states, the company has been successful in the application of new dialysis methodologies, research, and improving clinical outcomes and processes. Benefits realized through the Renal Research Institute may be applied to the entire worldwide Fresenius network of clinics.[51]

In addition to clinical dialysis services, the company also provides a wide range of support laboratory services. Through sites in Fremont, California, Rockleigh, New Jersey, and Chicago, Illinois, the laboratory business segment supported 1,461 dialysis clinics in 1999. As of 1999, the lab segment provided over 37 million tests and held approximately 37% of the market.[52] However, as large providers of dialysis add their own lab business units, the company's market share and tests performed may drop as the number of players increase in this market.

As its former primary business, Fresenius also manufactures dialysis machines, artificial kidneys, bloodlines, concentrates, dialysis chairs, and products for peritoneal dialysis.

Other Possible Merger Partners

For Everest, the list of other possible candidates of larger dialysis chains was fairly limited. One of the more aggressive consolidation companies, Total Renal Care, once a company that used a significant amount of equity to purchase several dialysis companies, was riddled with problems stemming from the over reporting of revenue. The stock price of the company fell dramatically ultimately resulting in the replacement of the CEO. As a result, at least in the short term, the company's ability to successfully purchase other dialysis companies was significantly reduced.

---

[51] Fresenius Medical Care. 1999 Annual Report.
[52] Fresenius Medical Care. 1999 Annual Report.

John D. Sullivan, Ph.D.

Conclusion

The Everest Healthcare Services Board of Directors had to make a decision soon. As the industry continued to rapidly consolidate, the longer they waited, the less leverage they would have in negotiating managed care contracts. However, given their present size, any problems with contract negotiations would be far off in the future. The board had once considered merging with Fresenius, but the time just didn't seem right. The question that remained was whether or not Fresenius was the correct match at the right time and if an appropriate purchase price could be reached.

Exhibit 1

Case Studies in Mergers & Acquisitions

Everest Healthcare Services

Payor Mix

Fiscal year ended September 30

PAYOR	1997	1998	1999
Chronic and Acute Dialysis:			
Medicare	57.50%	47.70%	49.90%
Medicaid	8.50%	7.40%	7.30%
Other payors	19.20%	30.60%	29.70%
Contract services:			
Hospitals and other payors	12.30%	12.50%	11.70%
Management service fees	2.50%	1.80%	1.40%
	100.00%	100.00%	100.00%

John D. Sullivan, Ph.D.
Exhibit 2

Everest Healthcare Services
Income Statements

	1995	1996	1997	1998	1999
		(in thousands)			
Statement of Operations Data:					
Net revenues	$47,276	$83,171	$113,808	$147,475	$184,918
Patient care cost	33,454	58,854	81,913	102,644	131,634
General and administrative expenses	10,577	13,494	14,855	23,286	24,328
Special charges	-	-	-	-	22,959
Provision for bad debts	754	2,523	714	2,727	7,360
Depreciation and Amortization	1,271	3,401	4,940	6,927	10,479
Income (loss) from operations	1,220	4,899	11,386	11,891	-11842
Interest expense, net	-368	276	2,148	5,932	11,084
Equity in earning of affiliates	-	-	-	1,784	586
Minority interest in earnings	-	-810	-1,601	-516	-843
Gain on curtailment of pension benefits	-	3,044	-	-	-
Other income, net	-	39	279	-	-
Income (loss) before income taxes and Cumulative effect of change in accounting	852	6,896	7,916	7,227	-23,183
Income tax expense (benefit)	325	2,800	3,689	3,541	-6,827
Income (loss) before cumulative effect of change in accounting	-	-	-	-	615
Net income (loss)	$527	$4,096	$4,227	$3,686	-16971

Exhibit 3

Case Studies in Mergers & Acquisitions

Everest Healthcare Services

Assets

(in thousands)

	1998	**1999**
Current Assets		
Cash & Equivalents	$12,526	$3,381
Patient Account Rec	$39,174	$47,411
Refundable Income Tax	$2,417	$3,008
Other Receivable	$2,971	$3,006
Medical Supplies Inventory	$2,812	$3,542
Deferred Income Tax	$3,152	$5,150
Prepaid expenses and other	$719	$311
Total Current Assets	$63,771	$65,809
Property and Equipment net	$27,735	$31,665
Goodwill net	$58,815	$73,448
Deferred Financing Cost	$6,112	$6,563
Other Intangible Assets net	$20,335	$2,671
Investments	$18,333	$8,902
Deferred Income Taxes		$5,998
Other Assets	$1,294	$1,217
Total Assets	$196,395	$196,273

John D. Sullivan, Ph.D.
Exhibit 4

Everest Healthcare Services

Liabilities & Stockholder Equity

(in thousands)

	1998	1999
Current Liabilities:		
Accounts payables	$8,845	$12,824
Accrued liabilities	16,849	17,206
Current portion of long-term debt	606	801
Current portion of capital lease obligation	506	367
Total current liabilities	26,806	31,198
Long term debt, less current portion	108,147	121,653
Capital lease obligation, less current portion	311	402
Deferred income taxes	1,500	-
Minority interest	1,375	1,735
Stockholders' equity:	13	13
Additional paid-in-capital	55,171	55,171
Retained earnings	3,072	-13,899
Total Stockholders' equity	58,256	41,285
	$196,395	$196,273

Exhibit 4

Everest Healthcare Services

Facilities

State	Facilities
Illinois	14
Indiana	9
Kansas	1
Kentucky	2
New Jersey	5
New York	8
Ohio	15
Oklahoma	2
Pennsylvania	1
South Dakota	2
Texas	8
Wisconsin	1
Total	**68**

John D. Sullivan, Ph.D.
Exhibit 5

Fresenius Medical Care

Segment Data

(in millions)

	1999	1998	1997
Total Revenue			
North America	$2,811	$2,565	$2,157
International	$1,076	$986	$867
Totals	$3,887	$3,551	$3,024
Intersegment Revenue			
North America	$4	$2	$1
International	$43	$43	$49
Totals	$47	$45	$50
Total Net Revenue			
North America	$2,807	$2,563	$2,156
International	$1,033	$943	$818
Totals	$3,840	$3,506	$2,974
EBITDA			
North America	$611	$549	$457
International	$243	$228	$192
Special Charge	($601)	$0	$0
Corporate	($10)	($9)	($8)
Totals	$243	$768	$641
EBIT			
North America	$394	$334	$258
International	$178	$165	$142
Special Charge	($601)	$0	$0
Corporate	($12)	($10)	($9)
Totals	($41)	$489	$391

Exhibit 6

Fresenius Medical Care

Income Statement

(in thousands)

	1999	1998	1997
Net Revenue			
Dialysis Care	$2,599,688	$2,358,577	$1,901,189
Dialysis Products	$1,240,741	$1,147,099	$1,073,180
Total Revenue	$3,840,429	$3,505,676	$2,974,369
Cost of Revenue			
Dialysis Care	$1,736,165	$1,568,192	$1,238,612
Dialysis Products	$688,438	$637,394	$647,874
Total Cost of Revenue	$2,424,603	$2,205,586	$1,886,486
Gross Profit	$1,415,826	$1,300,090	$1,087,883
Operating Expenses			
S,G,&A	$823,124	$779,962	$674,811
Research & Development	$32,488	$31,150	$22,136
Special Charge	$601,000	$0	$0
Operating Income	($40,786)	$488,978	$390,936
Interest Income	($8,094)	($8,641)	($10,312)
Interest Expense	$226,218	$228,182	$193,860
Income (loss)	($258,910)	$269,437	$207,388

John D. Sullivan, Ph.D.

Suggested Questions for Students

1. How well positioned in the market is Everest?

2. What would you consider is Everest's strengths and weaknesses?

3. What is Everest's most profitable segment and why?

4. How much is Everest worth?

5. If Fresenius purchases Everest, who assumes the long term debt? How should the long term debt be included into the purchase price?

6. Why might Everest reject an offer?

7. Is this a question of price or fit or both?

8. Would Everest be better off merging with a small to medium dialysis provider?

9. Does Everest have to merge with someone at this point?

10. Why is Fresenius so interested in Everest?

11. How does adding Everest to Fresenius improve Fresenius' operations?

12. If Total Renal Care's stock price has been suppressed, why not pursue this acquisition?

13. What synergies does Fresenius bring to the table? Should these be used to value Aetna?

14. Should Everest accept an offer by Fresenius? If you were on the Board, how would you vote?

15. Should the recent settlement by Fresenius with the Office of Inspector General have an impact on the Board's vote?

Laidlaw, Inc.

Background

Founded in 1924, Laidlaw had run solid for almost 75 years. But in 1999, the atmosphere changed for the Canadian corporation. Under an aggressive acquisition strategy that consumed the 1990s, along with growth in revenue came a heavy burden of long-term debt surpassing $3.1 billion. What had once been a profitable company reporting Net Income of $346 million in 1998 had experienced a reversal of fortune. For fiscal year ending August of 1999, Laidlaw's Net Income plunged to ($1.1) billion and for the nine months ending May of 2000, Net Income fell further to ($1.9) billion.[53]

As a short-term measure, management negotiated with bondholders to receive sufficient consents to permit certain subsidiaries to enter into secured banking agreements. The financing arrangements would provide a revolving line of credit in an amount up to $150 million with a letter of credit in amount up to $50 million from a group of financial institutions led by Canadian Imperial Bank of Commerce. In addition, a revolving line of credit would be available up to $125 million with a credit sub-facility in an amount up to $25 million for Greyhound Lines, Inc. from Foothill Capital Corporation, a wholly owned subsidiary of Wells Fargo.

The consent agreement, announced on October 25, 2000 in Dallas, Texas, only provides Laidlaw and Greyhound with a short-term solution to their financial problems. For the company to survive, it will need to implement a solid restructuring plan.

The Company

Laidlaw Inc. serves as a holding company and through operating its subsidiaries, provides essential and specialized services dedicated to the transportation of people throughout North America. Founded in 1924 by Robert Laidlaw, the company had built a reputation for waste management. But by the early

---

[53] Laidlaw – Investor Relations. www.laidlaw.com/laidlaw/investors/hls_three.html

1990's, through an acquisition and divestiture strategy (exhibit 1), the company became recognized for the yellow school buses that hold its name. Under the leadership of James Bullock, the company sold off non-core holdings and diversified into health care with the acquisition of American Medical Response for approximately $1.1 billion in 1997. That same year, Laidlaw added to its health care portfolio with the purchase of EmCare, an emergency room manager, for $400 million. Adding to the company's investment in waste management, Laidlaw purchased Safety-Kleen, a company specializing in hazardous waste management, in 1998 for $2 billion.

Under the umbrella of its core transportation business, Greyhound Canada was acquired in 1997. To compliment this merger, Laidlaw followed with the purchase of Greyhound Lines Inc., in 1999 for $800 million. Greyhound is the only nationwide provider of scheduled inter-city bus transportation services in the United States.

In the last three fiscal years, the percentage of revenue generated by the United States Operations has been 87.2%, 83.2% and 86.0%, respectively. The company intends to continue to expand throughout North America in each of its core businesses.[54]

Education Services

Laidlaw operates school buses and special education vehicles, primarily under the names Laidlaw Transit, Mayflower Contract Services, and National School Bus Services in the United States. In Canada, Laidlaw operates school buses under Laidlaw Transit and Charterways. Although Laidlaw purchased seven education service businesses in 1999, revenue growth was primarily attributable to price and volume growth including route additions and higher pricing on under performing contracts.

Laidlaw currently operates under 1,072 school boards in the United States and 61 in Canada providing transportation for approximately 2.3 million students each day. Contracts in the United States

---

[54] Laidlaw Inc., Securities and Exchange Form 10K. August 1999.

Case Studies in Mergers & Acquisitions

are generally three to five year agreements with options by the school board to extend the contracts or solicit new bids. In Canada, most contracts are one-year agreements and negotiated or renewed annually. Rates are usually established on a per-diem basis and vary with the number of buses and students and length of each route. In addition to the transportation of students, the school bus fleet is also utilized for charters.

Education services employs approximately 46,500 people to provide transportation services of which 2,800 provide executive, supervisory, clerical, and sales functions. Nearly 41,200 are considered part-time employees and approximately 47% are members of collective bargaining groups. The management of this division believes that management and work force have an excellent working relationship.

Transit and Tour Services

Laidlaw had acquired Greyhound Lines, Inc. during fiscal 1999 and had previously acquired Greyhound Canada Transportation Corp. in October 1997. Greyhound serves the "value-oriented" customer by offering scheduled passenger service that connects rural and urban markets throughout the United States and Canada with 3,700 destinations, 20,000 daily departures, and a fleet of approximately 2,500 buses. Greyhound also provides package express service, charter bus service, and in many terminals, food service. The company also provides services to municipal transit customers through 225 contracts in the United States and Canada. Additional services include para-transit services providing access to transportation for mobility impaired individuals, scheduled services under private contracts, and package tours to major tourist regions of the United States and Canada.

Approximately 24,800 people are employed to provide transit and tour services. Of these employees, 3,400 persons serve executive, supervisory, clerical, and sales functions. Nearly 5,400 employees are considered part-time and 9,900 are members of collective bargaining agreements. The Amalgamated Transit Union or ATU, represents 5,000 of Greyhound's employees. The largest ATU agreement, which covers drivers and mechanics, expires on January 31, 2004.[55]

[55] Laidlaw Inc., Securities and Exchange Form 10K. August 1999.

211

Greyhound's business is seasonal in nature and tends to peak during the summer months and major holidays. As a result, cash flows experienced by the company also tend to be seasonal.

Major Competitors in Education and Transit Services

Although Laidlaw is the largest school bus company and special education transport operator in North America, it competes directly with other large companies and a substantial number of small local operators including school districts and other municipalities that operate their own education transit system. When contracts with school boards expire, competition for extensions or new contracts is most prevalent in the areas of pricing and service.

The transportation industry is highly competitive and includes individual automobile usage, low cost air travel, regional bus companies, and the train system. Greyhound competes in this industry based on cost and convenience.

Coach USA Inc.

The largest bus charter service and the second largest bus company in the United States, Coach USA is operating under the restructuring plan of its United Kingdom parent Stagecoach Holdings. Coach USA provides airport ground transportation and daily routes to special destinations for commuters. The company's fleet consists of 9,500 buses, taxicabs, mini-coaches, and shuttle buses. Like Laidlaw, the company has fueled its rapid expansion through acquisitions and now operates in 35 states in the United States and throughout Canada.

First Group Plc.

First Group Plc., smaller than both Coach USA and Laidlaw, has taken advantage of Britain's deregulation of the bus, coach, train, and airport industries. The company operates several rail lines in the

Case Studies in Mergers & Acquisitions

UK and owns a 51% stake in the Bristol International Airport. As with Coach USA and Laidlaw, much of the company's growth has been achieved through acquisitions. One acquisition in particular, Ryder's bus division, has brought the company to the United States.

National Railroad Passenger Corporation (Amtrak)

National Railroad Passenger Corporation, or Amtrak, carries approximately 21 million passengers each year and operates 22,000 miles through 45 states in the US. A large "for-profit" company that has rarely been profitable receives subsidies through the United States federal government to ensure its operation. To lure passengers away from the lucrative shuttle flights on the East Coast, Amtrak has constructed a high-speed rail to open in 2000.

Southwest Airlines

Southwest Airlines has expanded its low cost, no frills, and no reserved seats approach to air travel to serve more than 55 cities and 29 states in the US. To curb maintenance and training expenditures, the airline uses only Boeing 737s and currently uses approximately 320 planes. To trim back office expenditures, Southwest offers ticketless travel and operates its own reservation system. As part of the airlines expansion plans, Southwest has increased its routes throughout the East Coast and continues to thrive with its highly participative corporate culture and 27 years of profitability.

Emergency Health Care Services

Laidlaw provides healthcare transportation services, primarily under the name American Medical Response, and emergency room management services under the name EmCare. In 1999, the company had announced plans to divest both of these operations.

The company provides health care transportation services from locations in 36 states in the United States and also operates in Ontario, Canada. These services consist of critical care transportation services, non-emergency ambulance and transfer services, and emergency response services. Annually, the company provides approximately five million ambulance responses and has more than 200 agreements with municipal or country public safety agencies to provide performance-based contracts for 911 responses. The company also provides comprehensive on-site medical care and transport services for all types of special events.

Laidlaw also offers physician practice management services to hospital based emergency departments. The company recruits physicians, evaluates their credentials, and arranges contracts and schedules for their services. The company also assists in such operational areas as staff coordination, quality assurance, departmental accreditation, billing, record keeping, third party payment, and other administrative services. Currently, Laidlaw has approximately 300 contracts for the management of emergency room departments and provides emergency services in 36 states to more than 5 million patients.

As a result of poor financial performance, Laidlaw announced in March 1999 that approximately 2,200 positions or 10% of this division's workforce would be eliminated. Under the restructuring plan, under performing locations would be closed or sold.

As of fiscal year end 1998, Laidlaw employed approximately 24,500 employees in the health care division. Of these, 5,200 employees are executive, clerical, supervisory, and sales. 5,900 employees are considered part-time and approximately 53% are members of collective bargaining agreements.

Major Competitors in Health Care Services

Laidlaw is the largest provider of health care transportation services in the United States and competes both with large companies and a substantial number of smaller operators. The primary competition with the renewal or extension of contracts is based on price and service performed.

Emergency physician practice management is also emerged in heavy competition. Competition for these contracts is usually based on cost and the ability to make physicians available as needed. In addition, competition is also based on maintaining the proper utilization and communication between the emergency room and other departments within the hospital.

American Medical Alert Corp.

American Medical Alert offers medical dispensing devices and fire burglar alarm monitoring. Nearly 95% of the company's sales come from monthly fees for leasing and monitoring its emergency response systems and other equipment. Primary customers for the service include individuals, hospitals, retirement homes, and the City of New York's Homecare Service Program.

Community Medical Transport, Inc.

Community Medical Transport provides medical transportation offering ambulance services for patients that require basic medical care or supervision during transport to or from hospitals, nursing homes in the New York metro area.

Rural Metro Corporation

Rural Metro provides ambulance, fire protection, and other safety related services to municipal, residential, commercial, and industrial customers in the United States. The large health care ambulance provider, second only to American Medical Response, responds to emergence calls and offers non-emergency transport between health care facilities. Fees collected for ambulance services account for more than 80% of sales. The company also provides municipal and commercial fire fighting services and provides training for fire fighters for industrial manufacturing facilities. Rural Metro operates in more than 450 communities in 26 states, Canada, and South America.

John D. Sullivan, Ph.D.

Med-Emerg International, Inc.

Med-Emerg International, Inc. is emerging as a player in Canada's medical industry. The company is divided into three primary divisions: Physician and Nurse Recruitment Services, Physician Management Services, and HealthyConnect.com, an online health care network. Med-Emerg International, Inc. owns clinics offering services such as family practice, emergency care, chiropractic care, massage therapy, Chinese medicine, and family counseling. The company also provides short-term physician and nurse staffing and administrative support to emergency room departments and hospitals. The company's web site is designed to link patients, physicians, and service providers.

PhyAmerica Physician Group, Inc.

PhyAmerica Physician Group, Inc. provides contract physicians primarily to emergency rooms to approximately 270 hospitals, government agencies, the military, the Veterans Administration, and correctional facilities. The company has refocused its attention to its main core contract business divesting businesses such as its HMO.

Other Business Segments

As of August 1999, Laidlaw owned approximately 44% of the shares of common stock of Safety-Kleen Corp. Safety-Kleen provides industrial waste services designed to collect, process, recycle and dispose of hazardous and industrial waste to more than 400,000 companies through over 200 locations. These services include collection and recovery services, provided to industrial, commercial and institutional customers and treatment and disposal services, defined by the technologies employed such as thermal treatment, landfill, and specialty services. On September 13, 1999, Laidlaw announced its plan to actively seek a buyer for its interest in Safety-Kleen.

Case Studies in Mergers & Acquisitions

In addition to financial under performance, Safety-Kleen has received several class action suits since April 2000 alleging that the company had accounting irregularities and may have misled investors. Following the suits, the company hired Lazard Freres & Co LLC for financial advice. In the meantime, three top executives were suspended in May 2000 as a result of the accounting irregularities and new management has been set in place to resolve any further issues with the company's financial reporting.

In October of 2000, Laidlaw sold its Manchu Wok Chinese food business to an investor group for an undisclosed amount. Manchu Wok is a chain of Chinese fast food restaurants that operates throughout North America, as well as two units in Poland.

Major Competitors in Waste Management
Allied Waste Industries, Inc.

Allied Waste Industries, Inc. collects trash and garbage from approximately 9.9 million residential and commercial customers throughout the United States. As the number two waste management operator behind Waste Management, Inc., the company participates in every facet of the non-hazardous waste industry through 150 transfer stations, 160 landfills, and 90 recycling facilities.

Republic Services, Inc.

As the number three waste collector, Republic Services, Inc. provides waste disposal services for commercial, industrial, municipal, and residential customers through 151 collection companies in 24 states in the United States and one in Canada. The company also operates 55 landfills and more than 80 transfer stations.

Waste Management, Inc.

Waste Management, Inc., formerly USA Waste Services, is the largest waste service provider in the United States. The company serves municipal, business, and residential customers in the United States,

Canada, and Mexico. Focusing on the company's core operations in North America, Waste Management is in the process of selling its solid and hazardous waste management services in Asia, Europe, the Pacific Rim, and South America.

Conclusion

Laidlaw is in a period of transition. Under an aggressive acquisition strategy, in addition to new divisions and base businesses, the company has added a significant amount of debt to its balance sheet. Under an agreement with its bondholders, the company has renewed hopes with a short-term financing agreement. However, for the company to survive, a restructuring plan must be set in place immediately. Otherwise, the only option available is bankruptcy protection.

Exhibit 1

The Evolution of Laidlaw

1924   Founded in Ontario, Canada as a trucking company by Robert Laidlaw

1959   Company sold to Michael DeGroote

1969   Company shares listed on the Toronto Stock Exchange
First Canadian solid waste management company acquired

1972   First Canadian intercity and charter bus company acquired

1978   First solid waste company acquired

1979   First Canadian school bus company acquired

1983   First US school bus company acquired
Stock is listed NASDAQ

1984   Trucking business sold

1986   Entered US chemical waste management business with acquisition

1988   Canadian Pacific Limited purchased

1989   Tricil acquired – chemical waste management business

1990   DeGroote Retires
Class A & B listed NYSE

1993   MedTrans acquired – Enters US ambulance business
James Bullock becomes new President

1994   USPCI acquired – Waste management business

1995   Mayflower acquired – US school bus and transit company
Care Line acquired – US ambulance business

1996   Charterways and National School Bus acquired
Solid Waste Management Units sold

1997   American Medical Response acquired
Laidlaw environmental sold
Stock restructured to one class
Greyhound Canada acquired
EmCare and Spectrum acquired

1998   Laidlaw invests in Safety Kleen

1999   Greyhound Lines, Inc. acquired
Sale of American Medical Response, EmCare & Safety Kleen announced

John D. Sullivan, Ph.D.
Exhibit 2

Acquisitions by Division

Nine Months Ended May 31

	2000	**1999**
Education Services	6	7
Transit & Tour Services	2	7
Total	8	14

Exhibit 3

Financial Statistics

52 Week Low (Nov 24, 00)	0.063
52 Week High (Jan 5, 00)	0.109
Beta	1.09
Daily Volume	729,000

John D. Sullivan, Ph.D.

Exhibit 4

Consolidated Balance Sheets

Assets

(in millions)

	31-May-00	31-Aug-99
Assets		
Current Assets		
Cash	$189	$58
Investments	$174	$209
Accounts Rec	$329	$215
Other	$96	$82
Total Current Assets	$788	$564
Net Assets Discontinued		
Operations	$505	$1,617
Long Term Investments		
Safety Kleen	$0	$593
Other	$206	$188
Total LT Investments	$206	$781
PP & E	$2,208	$2,112
Less Depr. Amort	$754	$632
Net PP & E	$1,454	$1,480
Other Assets		
Goodwill	$1,212	$1,212
Deferred Charges	$11	$31
Deferred Income Tax	$0	$68
Total Other	$1,223	$1,312
Total Assets	$4,177	$5,754

Exhibit 5

Consolidated Balance Sheets

Liabilities & Shareholder Equity

(in millions)

	31-May-00	31-Aug-99
Liabilities		
Current Liabilities		
Accounts Payable	$93.5	$139.4
Accrued Liabilities	$353.3	$337.2
Current Long Term Debt	$3,457.2	$9.3
Total Current Liabilities	$3,904.0	$485.9
Deferred Items	$166.9	$242.0
Long Term Debt	$197.9	$3,113.3
Shareholder Equity		
Preference Shares	$7.9	$8.0
Common Shares	$2,222.6	$2,246.8
Foreign Currency Translation	($167.6)	($168.4)
Deficit	($2,155.0)	($173.3)
Total Shareholders Equity	($92.1)	$1,913.1
Total Liabilities & Equity	$4,176.7	$5,754.3

John D. Sullivan, Ph.D.

Exhibit 6

Long Term Debt

As of August 1999 and August 1998)

(in millions)

	Maturity	Weighted Average Interest Rate 1999	Weighted Average Interest Rate 1998	Book Value 1999	Book Value 1998
Short Term	Less than one year	0.072	0.061	$9.3	$1.8
Long Term					
Bank Debt	2000-2005	0.055	0.054	$649.2	$454.8
Notes and Other	2000-2033	0.074	0.062	$137.3	$87.9
Debentures	2000-2027	0.074	0.076	$2,326.8	$1,747.3
Total Long Term Debt				$3,113.3	$2,290.0
Total Debt				$3,122.6	$2,291.8

Exhibit 7

Debt to Equity Ratio

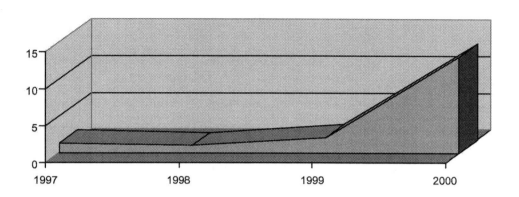

John D. Sullivan, Ph.D.
Exhibit 8

Income Snapshot

(in millions)

	31-May-00	**31-May-99**
Education Services		
Revenue	$1,255.1	$1,159.9
Income from Operations before Amortization	$188.1	$202.9
Income from Operations	$167.1	$183.6
Transit & Tour Services		
Revenue	$1,053.6	$530.2
Income from Operations before Amortization	$32.8	$26.4
Income from Operations	$19.8	$18.5

Exhibit 9

Case Studies in Mergers & Acquisitions

Laidlaw

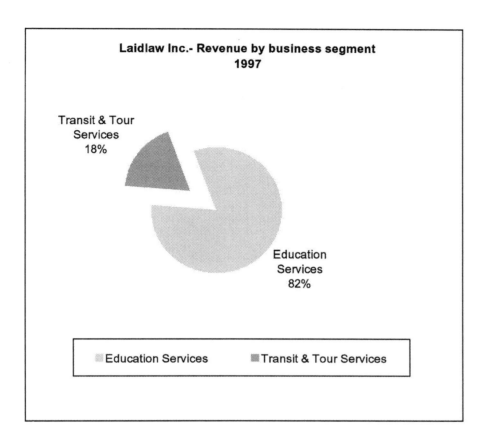

Sources of Revenue 1997

John D. Sullivan, Ph.D.
Exhibit 10

Laidlaw

Sources of Revenue 1999

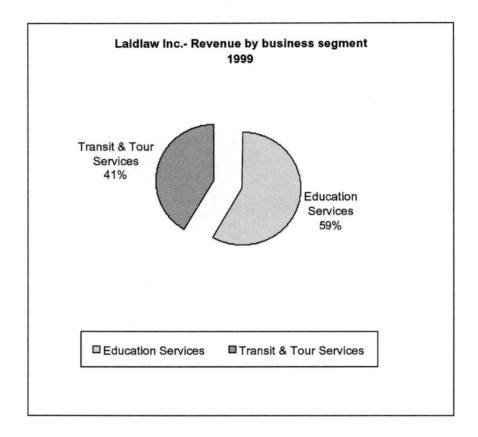

Exhibit 11

Laidlaw

Consolidated Statements of Operations

(in millions)

	Three Months Ended 31-May		Nine Months Ended 31-May	
	2000	1999	2000	1999
Revenue				
Education Services	$441.0	$414.8	$1,255.1	$1,159.9
Transit & Tour	$370.6	$301.0	$1,053.6	$530.2
Total Revenue	$811.6	$715.8	$2,308.7	$1,690.1
Operating Expenses	$581.8	$494.2	$1,637.2	$1,171.9
SG,& A	$94.8	$77.9	$273.7	$142.9
Depreciation	$60.2	$53.0	$176.9	$146.0
Amortization Expense	$14.8	$11.2	$34.0	$27.2
Income from Operations	$60.0	$79.5	$186.9	$202.1
Interest Expense	($56.6)	($27.0)	($134.3)	($60.4)
Other Financing	($89.0)	$0.0	($89.0)	$0.0
Other Income	$2.5	$13.8	$10.3	$56.2
Earnings Safety Kleen	$0.0	$10.8	$10.8	$27.3
Impairment Loss	($58.8)	$0.0	($663.8)	$0.0
Income Before Tax	($141.9)	$77.1	($679.1)	$225.2
Income Taxes	($1.5)	($16.6)	($15.8)	($49.5)
Tax Other	($85.0)	$0.0	($106.5)	($21.0)
Income\Loss from Op	($228.4)	$60.5	($801.4)	$154.7
Discontinued Operations	($314.1)	($287.7)	($1,148.6)	($278.7)
Net Loss for the Period	($512.5)	($227.2)	($1,950.0)	($124.0)

John D. Sullivan, Ph.D.
Exhibit 12

Laidlaw

EBITA by Business Segment 1997

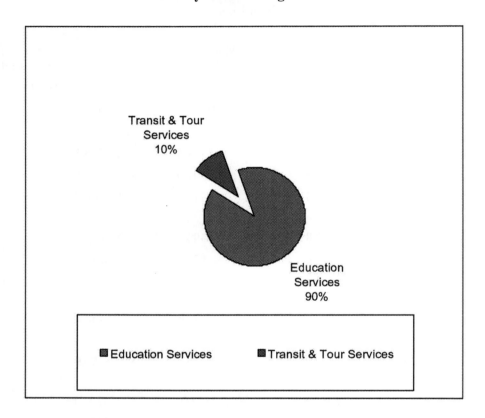

Exhibit 13

Laidlaw

EBITA by Business Segment 1999

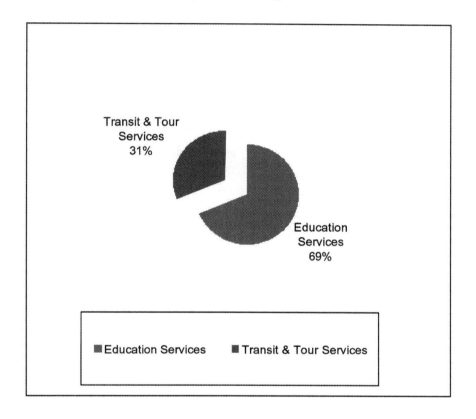

John D. Sullivan, Ph.D.
Exhibit 14

Stock Price History

Calendar Year	1999	1998	1997	1996	1995
High Price	$10.50	$16.63	$18.00	$12.25	$10.13
Low Price	$5.06	$8.63	$11.63	$8.88	$8.25
Year End Price	$5.25	$10.06	$13.63	$11.75	$9.88
High P/E	20.92	20.42	333.33	30.78	37.78
Low P/E	10.09	10.60	215.28	22.30	30.78
Year End P/E	10.46	12.36	252.31	29.52	36.85
Dividend Yield	5.33	2.58	1.47	1.62	1.62

Exhibit 15

Market Capitalization History

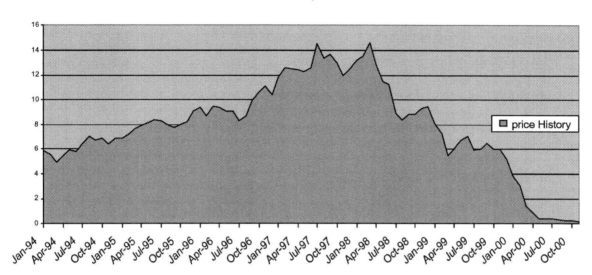

John D. Sullivan, Ph.D.

Suggested Questions for Students

15. How did Laidlaw weaken its financial strength?

16. Is Laidlaw's decision to sell its stake in Safety Kleen appropriate given Safety Kleen's legal troubles leading to filing for bankruptcy protection?

17. Given Safety Kleen's financial troubles, how much is it worth?

18. Why is Laidlaw selling its health care division?

19. How would you value the health care division?

20. Would Laidlaw be better off implementing and fulfilling its restructuring plan of the health care division?

21. How competitive is the health care market?

22. How strong are Laidlaw's Education, Transit, and Tourist Divisions?

23. Are these divisions strong enough to turn Laidlaw around?

24. What restructuring recommendations would you suggest in addition to the company's strategy of selling Safety Kleen and its health care unit.

25. How would the unions impact any of Laidlaw's restructuring plans? Does Laidlaw have sufficient time to turn the company around?

About the Author

John D. Sullivan, Ph.D.

Dr. Sullivan has over fifteen years of merger and acquisition experience participating in over 100 transactions. He holds a Ph.D. in Law and Public Policy from Northeastern University, a Masters from Harvard University, an MBA from Northeastern University, and a BA from Regis University. In addition to holding a faculty position at Boston University teaching Mergers & Acquisitions and Advanced Corporate Finance, he is a Principal at the consulting firm Genesis Capital Partners, LLC in Boston www.gencapllc.com. An avid sailor, he lives with his family on Boston's north shore.

In addition to several articles on the subject, he has published several novels, including Managed Care available through most retailers.